THE JOYFUL CHRIST

THE
JOYFUL
CHRIST

THE HEALING POWER
OF HUMOR

A fully revised and expanded edition of JESUS PUT ON
A HAPPY FACE ©1985 by Cal Samra.

Cal Samra

a rosejoy publication

1817

Harper & Row, Publishers, San Francisco

New York, Grand Rapids, Philadelphia, St. Louis
London, Singapore, Sydney, Tokyo, Toronto

For information regarding rosejoy contact rosejoy publications, an ecumenical lay fellowship, P.O. Box 668, Kalamazoo, Michigan 49005–0668.

Library of Congress Cataloging in Publication Data

Samra, Cal
   The Joyful Christ.

   "A rosejoy publication."
   Bibliography: p.
   1. Wit and humor—Religious aspects—Christianity. 2. Jesus Christ—Humor. 3. Joy—Religious aspects—Christianity. 4. Spiritual healing. I. Title.
BR115.H84S263   1986   241'.4   85–45366
ISBN 0-06-067032-0

90 91 92 93 94 95 MPC 20 19 18 17 16 15 14 13 12 11

For Rose, Paul, and Matt

"When you fast, do not put on a gloomy look as the hypocrites do."

(Matt. 6:16)

"I have told you this so that my own joy may be in you and your joy may be complete."

(John 15:11)

"If I can unite *in myself* the thought and devotion of Eastern and Western Christendom, the Greek and Latin Fathers, the Russians and the Spanish mystics, I can prepare in myself the reunion of divided Christians. From that secret and unspoken unity in myself can eventually come a visible and manifest unity of all Christians. If we want to bring together what is divided, we cannot do so by imposing one division upon the other. If we do this, the union is not Christian. It is political and doomed to further conflict. We must contain all divided worlds in ourselves and transcend them in Christ."*

Thomas Merton

---

*Excerpt from *Conjectures of a Guilty Bystander* by Thomas Merton. Copyright © 1965, 1966 by the Abbey of Gethsemani. Reprinted by permission of Doubleday & Company, Inc.

"But of a sudden I heard Mary say, 'My son, who is not my son, what have you said to the man at your right hand that has made him happy in his agony? The shadow of death is light upon his face, and he cannot turn his eyes from you.

" 'Now you smile upon me, and because you smile I know you have conquered.'

"And we came close to her, and she said to us, 'Even in death He smiles. He has conquered. I would indeed be the mother of a conqueror.' "*

—Kahlil Gibran

*Excerpt from *Jesus the Son of Man* by Kahlil Gibran. Copyright © 1928 by Kahlil Gibran and renewed 1956 by Administrators of Kahlil Gibran Estate. Reprinted by permission of Alfred A. Knopf, Inc.

CONTENTS

THE GOSPEL ACCORDING TO ERMA BOMBECK

Columnist Erma Bombeck and Father Tom Walsh, who has taught a course called "Humor, Hilarity, Healing, and Happy Hypothalami," have known each other for years, having met at St. Thomas the Apostle Church in Phoenix, Arizona. Father Tom wrote Mrs. Bombeck not long ago and asked whether she thinks humor is healing.

Mrs. Bombeck replied with a delightful letter. Here it is:

Dear Father Tom:

I suspect you have me confused with Norman Cousins. He's several inches taller, and he laughed his way through illness. He got a best-seller out of his illness. I got three children. Those are the breaks.

I am a great believer in your premise that humor heals. I have nothing to back it up physically, but emotionally I have file drawers of pure testimonials.

I've always wanted to teach a course on marriage, because you could pretty well judge who is going to survive a short wife who puts the car seat up under the steering wheel and never puts it back, and who refuses to put it back.

I've had pitiful letters from people who swear they don't have a sense of humor and want to know how to develop one, because they've heard how much of a stabilizer one is. And they're right.

What I have been doing for sixteen years in my column is to put my life in perspective, the frustration of raising children, the loneliness, the pain, and the futility of it all. And it works.

Last week, I got a great letter from a woman celebrating her fiftieth wedding anniversary. She said a lot of young people wondered how it lasted so long. She wrote: "For years, Herb and I both lusted after the cauliflower in the mixed pickle jar. Herb does not know this—I've always let him have the cauliflower."

One of the favorite stories I used to tell when I lectured was the Supermom who is perfection itself. She did everything right: kept a perfect home; kept her husband happy. Always had a copy of Bishop Fulton Sheen's latest book on the coffee table. And answered the door pregnant when the priest came by.

One day, I asked her how she did it, and she said: "I emulate the Blessed Virgin Mary," and I said, "Marge, it's a little bit late for that."

She said, "Very well, I'll tell you. Every evening, when the children are bathed and tucked into their clean little beds, and the lunches are lined up and labeled and packed in the refrigerator, and the little shoes are racked up, and the driveway is waxed, and I've heard all of the prayers of the children, I fall down on my knees and say, "Thank you, God, for not letting me kill one of them today."

I would see an auditorium of women breathe a sigh of relief.

Good luck. I miss you a lot at St. Thomas. Was it something I said?

HOW DO YOU HANG YOURSELF FROM A CACTUS?

One sunny morning three years ago, I was in the depths of depression and despair, burned out at the tender age of fifty. Everything that could go wrong had gone wrong in my life. My marriage had fallen apart. My health had greatly deteriorated, forcing me to resign my job in Michigan as a newspaper reporter and go to the warmer climate of Arizona, two thousand miles away from my children, relatives, and friends. I was jobless, looked like skin and bones, and in great emotional and physical pain. I was full of bitterness, anger, self-hatred, fear, and doubt. An urge to be finished with the pain overwhelmed me one day.

I went to a hardware store, bought some sturdy clothesline rope, and drove all over Phoenix and the surrounding desert looking for a suitable tree to hang myself from. But the Phoenix area has very few trees, and what trees they have are unsuitable for hanging. The palm trees are much too tall to climb, and most everything else is excruciatingly prickly cactus.

I finally drove into the desert near the elegant town of Carefree, sat in the sun next to a very tall cactus, and for a couple hours tried to figure out how to hang myself from it. How do you hang yourself from a cactus?

Finally, I decided that it was all very ridiculous, and that there was no way it could be done—not from a cactus. So I drove around looking for a river to jump into. But all of Arizona's rivers were dry that time of year, with not a drop of water in them.

Then I drove over to Scottsdale and stopped off at La Casa de Paz y Bien, the Franciscan Renewal Center. Something drew me into the chapel, where I found myself down on my knees, praying for the strength to endure my pain and to go on in spite of it.

I have dim memories of that day. But I remember Franciscan Father Gavin Griffith, a warm-hearted Irish wit who could have made a living as a stand-up comedian had he chosen to do so, inviting me to share a meal with him at the center. At dinner, Griffith had me laughing again with his pithy remarks and jokes. I remember seeing hanging from a wall in the kitchen a drawing of Jesus titled "The Laughing Christ," the first such portrayal I had ever seen.

I decided to take a few days' retreat at the center and had the good fortune of getting as a spiritual adviser Franciscan Father Lambert Fremdling, a small, gentle, German friar who had lived and worked for forty years on an Indian reservation in Arizona. He was a good-humored, elderly man who was a great believer in the siesta.

"If a person has prayed on a problem and it still doesn't go away, I suggest that they take a siesta and sleep on it," he said. "A siesta relaxes you. It puts distance between you and a problem. It renews you."

When the retreat was just about over, Father Lambert told me he had something he wanted to give me, and he went scurrying to his office. Soon he returned and gave me a painting of a smiling Christ carrying the imprint "Christ:

the Essence of Life, Light, Love, and Laughter." He said it had been painted by one of his friends, Mrs. Joyce Martin, of Montrose, Colorado, and he wanted me to have it.

The two modest prints of smiling Christs that I found at the Franciscan Renewal Center represented a turning point in my life. They gave me a different perspective on Jesus and cast him in a new light. This new vision of the joyful Christ is the portrait I would like to share with you.

Christians are a contentious bunch, and Paul complained that they were shooting down their own soldiers even back in the days of the apostles. We are forever praying for Christian unity and talking of the ecumenical spirit, while denominations continue to divide and multiply, and few practical gestures are made toward unity. In my case, however, it took an ecumenical effort to put this Humpty-Dumpty back together.

The effervescent and good-humored friars and sisters at the Franciscan Renewal Center in Scottsdale showed me how to reach out again to other people, to love again, and to laugh again. I am indebted to Father Tom Walsh, a Scottsdale counselor and humorist, and one of the people who inspired this book. I am also greatly indebted to Franciscan Father Jack Wintz, associate editor of *St. Anthony Messenger* magazine, for his patience in helping me put together an article called "Jesus Put on a Happy Face" for the September 1983 issue of that magazine; as well as to Franciscan Father Martin Wolter of the Alverna Retreat Center in Indianapolis for his spiritual and editorial advice.

I am also indebted to our Franciscan friend John Michael Talbot, the extremely talented singer and composer, who greeted me with warmth and hospitality when I stopped at his hermitage en route to Phoenix. I was a very depressed and sick man when I met this saintly young lay brother. A busy man, Talbot took the time to listen patiently to me and to encourage me.

In July 1983, my children and I stopped off to see Talbot in Eureka Springs, Arkansas, where he is constructing a Franciscan monastery. By this time, my health and spirits had greatly improved, and Talbot's first remark to me was, "So you've discovered the healing power of humor, have you?"

Talbot himself has a delightful sense of humor, and he likes to clown around with his friends. My wife, Rose, was the manager of his Indianapolis concert for the poor in the fall of 1983, and Talbot often touched the audience with his wit; for instance, modifying Augustine's famous remark as follows: "He who sings *well* prays twice."

It was through John Michael that Rose and I met, and we will always be indebted to him for the joy, as well as the music, he has brought into our lives.

I would like to thank many others:

• Father Norman Muckerman, editor of *The Liguorian* magazine, for his wit and wisdom and for publishing much of the material in Chapter 3, "Fools for Christ's Sake," in the January 1985 issue of that magazine.

• Presbyterian theologian Conrad Hyers, Baptist Pastor Tal D. Bonham, and Msgr. Arthur Tonne for the holy humor they've shared with me.

• Sister Mary Bader, of the Sisters of St. Joseph at Nazareth in Kalamazoo, Michigan; Carmelite Sister Marie-Celeste of Carmel of Reno, Nevada; and Marilyn Hood and the Sondancers for their infectious joy and for the materials they gave me on the Christian clown ministry.

• Francis MacNutt, director of Christian Healing Ministries,

Inc., of Clearwater, Florida, for his healing prayers, encouragement, and support. MacNutt is a very kind and gentle man who always responds quickly to people in need.

• Father Michael St. Andrew of St. Elias Eastern Orthodox Catholic Church in Battle Creek, Michigan, for his marvelous jokes and for teaching me the spiritual disciplines of prayer and fasting.

• Rev. Canon Alfred Price of St. Petersburg, Florida, and Rev. Henry Getz of Sun City, Arizona—two light-hearted Episcopalian priests who have been wardens of the Order of St. Luke—for the insights into Christian healing they have given me.

• Dr. Ken Olson, a Lutheran pastor and clinical psychologist in Phoenix, who never charged me a dime for counseling sessions when I was sick and broke, and who kept insisting that God is a humorist.

• Father Edward Griesemer, SCJ, formerly of St. Joseph Catholic Church, Battle Creek, a man with a large heart who isn't afraid to reach out to strangers.

• Dr. Doug Adams, a United Church of Christ minister who chairs the Christianity and Arts Department at the Pacific School of Religion in Berkeley, California, for the treasury of Protestant humor he has mined and shared.

Whatever their theological differences, each of these clergy and lay people reflected Christ in a different way, but they all shared in common a keen sense of humor.

My gratitude, also, to the following artists:

• Larry Zink, art director of *St. Anthony Messenger*, for the Smiling Christ he painted to illustrate my magazine article.

• Robert Lentz, staff artist of *The New Oxford Review* and one of America's foremost iconographers, for his keen observations on Orthodox iconography.

• Joyce Martin, of the Franciscan family retreat center in Montrose, Colorado, who saw Jesus in the faces of her husband and children and painted what she saw.

• Photographer Ameen Howrani of Detroit for his work with the illustrations.

No book ever has a single author. Everyone who has ever known or advised or informed or instructed or loved an author (however unlovable he or she may be at times) is in some way—knowingly or unknowingly—a contributor to the published book. I have been poor in many ways, but I have been blessed with the richness of friends. I discovered that, when you are down and out and you pray for help, the Lord never fails to send people to you who will cheer and lift you up. But God does not always send the people you expect.

In Phoenix, God sent me Lou Berman, a devout and merry-hearted Jew who became my doubles partner at Encanto Park. Lou is seventy-three, but he's been playing tennis—good tennis—on two artificial hips for more than ten years, even though he is often in pain. His unfailing cheerfulness, keen sense of humor, kindness, and courage were a source of great inspiration to me. "I've seen a lot of guys drive down to Phoenix in $30,000 Cadillacs and drive back in $150,000 Greyhound buses," he is fond of saying.

At another time when I needed a lift, the Lord sent me a gentle and good-humored Moslem doctor, Dr. Ali Ismailoglu, who always gave the same sound advice, which I often foolishly ignored: "Don't hurry, don't worry, and don't forget to stop and smell the roses." Dr. Ali is one of a number of physician friends, including Dr. Humphry Osmond and Dr. Abram Hoffer, who understand that humor can be a powerful ally of the competent medical doctor.

I have found in my pilgrimage that God uses many in

struments of healing: medical doctors, clergy, monks and religious women, charismatic laymen and women, singers, clowns, humorists, etc.

Space does not permit me to list all the people I would like to thank. My thanks to Sister Mary Laurentina, RSM, for helping to educate a slow-learning infant in basic Christianity. For their assistance in the preparation of this manuscript, my gratitude to Sandy and Mark Delorey, Conne Gormley, and Dr. Dick Means of the sociology department at Kalamazoo College. I also was blessed with the advice of Dr. Rozanne Elder, editorial director of Cistercian Publications in Kalamazoo.

I salute all the good and loving people in Dr. Ken Olson's prayer and healing community at Gloria Dei Lutheran Church in Paradise Valley, Arizona; at the Channel of Peace charismatic community in Indianapolis; at the Immaculate Heart of Mary Catholic Church in Indianapolis, where Father Jim Byrne presides with his Irish wit; at St. Elias Eastern Orthodox Catholic Church in Battle Creek; and at the charismatic prayer group at St. Catherine of Siena Church in Kalamazoo. Thanks for your prayers. They were answered.

Kudos to you, Erma Bombeck, for your permission to reprint your choice letter to Father Tom, and for the delightful tale from *At Wit's End*.

Thanks to my sons, Paul and Matt Samra, who have given me great joy and more laughs than I can remember.

Special thanks to my wife, Rose, for her love, support, good humor in the face of poverty, and her wonderful, smiling Irish eyes.

And thank God for his patience with, and mercy to, a long-standing sinner who is always messing up.

The author's opinions expressed in this book do not

necessarily reflect the views of any of the persons or publications acknowledged here, and their views are not necessarily mine.

This is an ecumenical book. It is not easy, I discovered, to write an ecumenical book. It seems these days that everyone wants to put you in a denominational box, as if Christ can be contained within the walls of one church. I am not a theologian, and I am far removed from being a biblical scholar or an authority on anything. I am often dazzled by my own ignorance and the colossal mystery of life. All I know is that Jesus *commanded* us (he didn't ask us) to love everyone—both believers and nonbelievers; to forgive quickly, as he forgave quickly; to be at peace and one in spirit with all Christians; and to reflect his joy.

A lot of contemporary books create divisions among Christians. I have tried to write a book that will contribute, if only in a small way, to the Christian unity which so many of us in all denominations yearn for but which keeps eluding us. My prayer is that this book will knock down a few walls and help heal a few wounds.

I believe that churches, as well as individuals, must learn to forgive in order to experience the Lord's healing. The day may come when Jesus will ask each of us: What did you *do* to divide my Church? What did you *do* to unify my Church? I believe the Lord is now saying to us all: Unify my Church. And I believe that when the divisions among Christians are healed, there will be a spectacular outpouring of healings throughout the world on a scale not seen since the early centuries of Christianity.

It is my belief that what scrupulous theology and bigotry divide, love and humor can unite.

The way of a Christian pilgrim may be a hard one sometimes, but it is not all sorrowing and lamentations, trials and temptations and tribulations, sufferings, groaning and gnashing of teeth, madness, and fierce spiritual warfare.

We also are surprised to find love, forgiveness, peace, mercy, joy, laughter, and hilarity along the way.

Peace, joy, and every blessing.

Cal Samra
April 1985

PART I

The Healing Power of Joy and Humor

Chapter 1

WHERE ARE ALL THE
JOYFUL CHRISTIANS?

On a wall in the kitchen of the Franciscan Renewal Center in Scottsdale, Arizona, hangs a drawing of Jesus titled "The Laughing Christ." It shows Jesus with his head thrown back and his mouth wide open, enjoying a hearty laugh.

A priest took the drawing and showed it to an adult education class. One rather grim-faced woman rose and asked, "Where in the Bible does it say that Jesus ever laughed?"

"Jesus was once a baby," the priest replied, "and presumably he wet his pants on occasion. Where in the Bible does it say he ever wet his pants?"

The woman walked out in a huff.

It is really surprising how many Christians cannot tolerate the image of a joyful, laughing Jesus. It is almost as if they prefer to contemplate the sorrowful Jesus of the Garden of Gethsemane and the tormented Jesus of the cross.

Recently, the Gallup Poll reported that Americans are about equally divided on whether Jesus was fun loving or somber. Now I happen to love both the weeping Jesus and the joyful Jesus, and I believe that God loves equally the saint who dances with joy and the saint who weeps over the sins of humanity. But I wonder sometimes whether we focus too much on the sorrowful Jesus.

Throughout the centuries, religious artists have rendered many representations of Christ in the icons and art of all Christian traditions. Christ has been portrayed variously as sorrowful, in great agony, tender and gentle of countenance, angry, stern, full of love and compassion, triumphant.

He was all of these. But very rarely, and only recently, has he been shown smiling or laughing.

English artist Curtis Hooper spent seven years researching Christ's physical appearance, and after enhancing hundreds of photographs of the image on the Shroud of Turin, he painted a portrait of Jesus that appeared in the February, 1984 issue of *Life* Magazine. His is a strong, gentle, appealing Christ, but not a smiling Christ. But Hooper concluded, after his research, that Jesus "was the world's most balanced man." I share that view. I would add that the most balanced people I know possess a certain quality of joy, have a keen sense of humor, and laugh with the easy spontaneity of a small child. The unbalanced rarely show joy or flashes of humor. Humor is a balancing, disarming, and therefore peacemaking force that touches on the divine.

Erma Bombeck wrote in her book *At Wit's End*, "I've taken a few lumps in my time for daring to smile at religion." Joel Wells, a Catholic satirist, observes that "when it comes to religion, anything that attempts to be even mildly amusing threatens closed minds. I've never figured out why. I grant that some attempts at humor are tasteless, that some cross the line into blasphemy, but I'm not talking

---

For the past couple of years, I have been collecting, where I can find them, paintings and drawings of smiling and laughing Christs. They are hard to come by. I have located only about a dozen so far, all of them done in recent years.

I am glad others share my view that if Jesus was "a man of sorrows and acquainted with grief," he was also a man of joy and acquainted with humor.

about attacks on the truly sacred. The veil of the sacred seems to cover everything associated with religion, and that veil shelters all manner of pomposities, absurdities, and just plain baloney—all of which are legitimate targets for humor."

Humor is a gift to the church, but there are people in all churches who would discourage and suppress it. I remember a few years ago having lunch with a friend who is a member of a small, rather humorless Protestant denomination. He got angry and walked away, leaving his meal unfinished, when I suggested that Christ laughed and enjoyed playing with children. Recently, the editor of a Catholic publication told me, gloomily, that he had found only one place in the New Testament where Jesus *may* have laughed.

Not long after his lady love tired of his gloominess and left him for another man, the melancholy nineteenth-century Danish philosopher, Søren Kierkegaard wrote that Christianity is not glad tidings to the unserious because it seeks to make them serious. The relentless seriousness of much of the Christianity of Kierkegaard's time as well as our own has put off a lot of potential converts.

Some Christians I know would not find anything funny about the following story, which actually happened: In one Sunday school class, some little children were asking where God lives. "He lives in our bathroom," a small boy said. "My dad bangs on the bathroom door every morning and says, 'My God, are you still in there?' "

Considering the fact that Christians have been raised to celebrate a "Merry Christmas" and a "Happy Easter," I have always wondered why Christian humorist-writers are as rare as desert penguins. Only a few names, like C. S. Lewis and Malcolm Muggeridge, come to mind.

An Episcopalian priest once told me that when he was

in seminary, one of his professors told the class that there "were two requirements to become a bishop: (1) gray hair to give you that distinguished look; and (2) hemorrhoids to give you that sorrowful look." But the truth is, in the history of the church there have been many merry-hearted and witty bishops, and we'll be introducing you to some of them in the pages to come.

Some Christians (of all denominations) have taken pride in their long-faced gloominess, and their relentless melancholia has driven a lot of potential converts away from church, to the great glee of the Devil. I know a nice young woman in Indianapolis who says she never goes to church because she finds it depressing.

Centuries of persecution and suffering have produced among Jews and Blacks a flock of humorists, comedians, and clowns—gifts from God to comfort the wounded. Joseph Boskin, writing in *Bostonia, Insight*, observes, "Jews and Blacks share deeply the humor of the oppressed; much of their laughter emanates from a history of intense discrimination. . . . The laughter of the oppressed has always resounded within their own communities."

But Christians, too, have a long history of persecution and discrimination. Periodically throughout two thousand years, Christians have suffered terrible persecutions, massacres, and martyrdoms at the hands of the Pharisees, pagan Romans, Turks, Moslems, Nazis, Communists, and, I might add, fellow Christians. Surely, the early Christians—hunted like animals—must have developed a keen sense of humor and the ability to laugh at their befuddled tormentors.

I can sympathize with the sensitivity of some Christians toward humor. Not all humor is good humor, and people have a right to object to tasteless humor. At times laughter is gauche or inappropriate. Some humor edifies and lifts people up; other humor humiliates and puts people down. There is joyful humor and joyless humor. There is a humor of love, which is healing, and a humor of hate, which is destructive. There is healthy humor and sick humor.

But how many Christians can tell you what Jesus said at the Last Supper? On the very eve of his crucifixion, Jesus admonished his disciples: "These things I have spoken to you, that my *joy* may be in you, and that your *joy* may be full" (John 15:11).

Joy!

Here is a man about to be arrested, tried, cursed, beaten, spit upon, humiliated, crucified, and he's talking about *joy*!

The Gospel writers faithfully noted the words of Jesus, but they did not record in writing things like the twinkle in the eye, the gentle smile, the grin, the hearty laugh, the tone and inflection of voice, the hand gestures.

Jesus said and did a lot of things the Gospel writers didn't record. The Apostle John makes this patently clear in the conclusion to his Gospel: "There are still many other things that Jesus did, yet if they were written about *in detail*, I doubt there would be room enough in the entire world to hold the books to record them" (John 21:25). The Gospels therefore are an incomplete record of the life of Jesus. Though the Gospel writers gave us the essentials of the life and teachings of Jesus, sufficient to ensure salvation for those who follow them, the personality of Jesus is not completely laid out in the Gospels.

It would be impossible for mere human beings, however inspired by the Holy Spirit, to put down in writing everything pertaining to the personality of a man who is the Messiah, the Son of God, who created everything and is in all creation, including joy and humor. Jesus' personality touched every person who came in contact with him.

The gospel literally means "the Good News," and messengers of good news are not ordinarily gloomy. It is only the messengers of bad news (some media reporters fit the description) who are inclined to be gloomy and cynical.

But would the multitudes have followed a gloomy Messiah?

We know that Jesus loved children, who laugh frequently and spontaneously. And I suspect that he, too, must have laughed frequently, not only at the foibles of the authorities, but also at the bumblings of his all-too-human disciples, who were missing the point and messing things up from time to time.

Not long ago, a friend of mine was married in an Orthodox wedding. His father, a retired priest in his eighties, assisted in the wedding ceremony. In mid-ceremony, when the frail old priest reached up to place the gold crown on his son's head, his suspenders snapped off and his pants fell in a heap at his feet, only partially covered by his vestments. Had Jesus been a guest at this wedding, I suspect that, like the rest of us, he would have found it exceedingly difficult to stifle a laugh.

Each of us has a different image of Jesus, and perhaps all of them are valid in some way. But it is my belief that although he wept on occasion over the sins and sufferings of humanity, Jesus before the crucifixion was joyful, and the resurrected Christ shone with the joy of the divine light.

The Humorist As Healer

There is another reason why I am convinced that Jesus had a divine sense of humor. Jesus was a healer, a proven physician and the greatest psychiatrist of all time. The most effective healers I have known were men and women with a keen sense of humor, for humor is healing. I think Jesus, being both divine and fully human and sharing with humanity a wide range of emotions, must also have used his sense of humor in his healing ministry.

Is it conceivable that Jesus, the divine healer, was not aware of Prov. 17:22: "A cheerful heart is a good medicine, but a downcast spirit dries up the bones"?

I once served as executive director of New York's Huxley Institute, which has been heavily engaged in psychiatric research. I thus developed a passing acquaintance with the hundreds of solemn and complex theories regarding various ailments and disturbances. I was delighted when one of the Institute's trustees, the eminent editor Norman Cousins, wrote a best-selling book, *The Anatomy of an Illness*, which described how he had healed himself by laughing his way through a supposedly incurable illness—watching old Laurel and Hardy, Marx Brothers, and Candid Camera movies.

One must never underestimate the power of humor. As Mark Twain once observed: "Against the assault of humor, nothing can stand."

A friend, Dr. Ken Olson, a Lutheran pastor and clinical psychologist in Paradise Valley, Arizona, says he often uses humor to help break up depression and reduce anxiety among his patients. "God is a humorist," claims Olson. "If you have any doubts about it, look in the mirror."

Father Tom Walsh, a Scottsdale, Arizona, psychotherapist, notes that while there are a multitude of emotional, physiological, and nutritional factors involved in depression, many of his clients have one thing in common: They take themselves and the world too seriously.

Bil Keane, syndicated cartoonist and creator of "Family Circus," wrote: "My friends Erma Bombeck and Art Buchwald have done far more for the health of humanity than Madame Curie or Dr. Christiaan Barnard.''

If Norman Cousins, Ken Olson, Tom Walsh, Bill Keane, Erma Bombeck, and Art Buchwald understand the healing power of humor, are we to suppose that Jesus Christ did not?

Humor, of course, is only one of many healing tools, but I think it is quite likely that Jesus used a gentle kind of humor in his approach to the ill and disturbed. His healthy, healing humor comforted the afflicted; but Jesus' wit afflicted the comfortable.

There are those who feel uncomfortable with humor, and feel that it is somehow irreverent. But we need not see humor and true religion as antagonistic.

Humor reminds us of our fragility, our weakness, our humanity. It teaches us not to take ourselves too seriously. It helps us learn humility. Humor is threatening only to the proud, the self-righteous, and the pharisaical, who even today are inclined to want to crucify people who express joy and wit.

Some of the most devout people I know have a keen sense of humor. The best jokes I've heard have been passed on to me by priests, friars, nuns, ministers, and rabbis. Among my favorites are actual letters to pastors from very small children that have been collected over the years:

"Dear Pastor: I know God loves everybody, but he never met my sister."

"Dear Pastor: Please say a prayer for our Little League team. We need God's help or a new pitcher."

"Dear Pastor: My mother is very religious. She goes to bingo every week."

Many Catholics wear religious medals around their necks, with these words inscribed on the back: "I am a

Catholic. In case of an accident, call a priest." When a Jesuit priest in New York was ordained, a group of nuns bought him a medal with this inscription: "I am a Catholic priest. In case of an accident, call a doctor."

And how about this one? A lawyer and a preacher died at the same time and went to heaven. St. Peter gave the preacher a small room, but he gave the lawyer a large suite. The preacher complained that he had served the Lord faithfully all his life and deserved a larger room.

"My dear Reverend," Peter explained, "we have lots of preachers up here. But he's the first lawyer we've ever had."

The Lord's Last Laugh

Like Jesus, the early Christians were widely known for their joyous and gentle spirit in the face of adversity and persecution. Their focus was less on the sorrow of the crucifixion than on the joy of the resurrection and the joy of life in Christ.

Christ came to us bringing peace, love, joy, laughter, and healing. And when he returns again, he will lead his disciples in a chorus of laughter, because, as the old saying goes, the Devil can't stand the sound of laughter. Christ will lead the disciples, the wounded and broken-hearted, in laughing away all the hypocrites, the greedy, the cruel, and all those who think they can hurt other people and get away with it. We will all join Christ in laughing away the false doctrines and pompous theories of our times. He will help us laugh away our despair, our hatred, vindictiveness, fear, anxiety, and depression, and all the things that make people sick in their souls. He will laugh away the barriers among Christians and between Christians and unbelievers. All will be blown away with divine laughter.

One day I saw a bumper sticker on a car in Phoenix, Arizona. It read, "God is simply fun." Few of us are accustomed to thinking of God in that way. But if God is a God of love and a God of peace and a God of joy, God also must be a God of fun.

If we walk with Jesus and weep with him, I think he also wants us to laugh with him. And have some fun. So let's have some fun.

The well-known Christian healer, Francis MacNutt, the author of several best-selling books, including *The Power to Heal*, believes that the church must recapture the healing ministry of the early Christians if it is to grow and be a credible witness in the modern world. MacNutt believes that we have to develop a more positive image of God. We need to see God as a loving, compassionate, forgiving Father who heals us through human instruments—clergy, doctors and inspired lay people, a God who laughs as well as weeps, a God who wants every one of us to laugh and to be happy.

Chapter 2

THE DEVIL CAN'T STAND
THE SOUND OF LAUGHTER

We are almost to the very end of the sophisticated and troubled twentieth century, and some health professionals are only now discovering what the Bible and the Church's saints told us centuries ago: that love, joy, and humor have great healing power.

Dr. Raymond Moody of Atlanta, Georgia, author of *Laugh after Laugh* and a physician who says he hopes some day to become a stand-up comedian, described how he has tried to apply humor in his psychiatric practice.

"I've been amazed by how many professional clowns will tell you . . . where they've been able to go into hospitals and bring back people who are just terribly despondent—so despondent that they hadn't talked in a long time. These things do take place. Why? I'm not sure."

Moody said he was once counseling "a very, very depressed" man in a psychiatric clinic. "I was biting the insides of my cheeks, trying to look appropriately profound," Moody recalls, "and all these things were going through my mind—like, you know, the voices of my supervisors saying, 'Never laugh at a psychiatric patient; you'll precipitate a psychotic breakdown.' And then he [the patient] looked at me and he started smiling, kind of, and then he started laughing . . . and laughing and laughing. We both laughed so hard! And from that point the therapy really started progressing."

Moody believes "humor can make us better by enabling us to stand aside from things."

My old friend, Dr. Humphry Osmond, an internationally famous psychiatrist and researcher into the biological and nutritional factors involved in psychiatric disorders, has long been one of the most persistent advocates of good cheer and humor in medicine. In the early 1960s, Dr. Osmond, who was then director of psychiatric research for the state of New Jersey, his associate, Dr. Abram Hoffer, of Victoria, British Columbia, and I organized what was to become New York's Huxley Institute to fund research on various psychiatric disorders, including conditions described as schizophrenia, manic-depression, depression, infantile autism, and alcoholism.

This was serious business. But what I remember most in my six years as executive director of the foundation was not all the grave and melancholy psychiatric research papers, journals, and books I had to pore over and the solemn lectures I had to sit through. I remember little of that, thank God. What did make an indelible impression on my mind was the wit and humor of Dr. Osmond, now professor of psychiatry at the University of Alabama in Birmingham.

Osmond faithfully chronicles the ailments of his late friends, the English biologist-geneticist Sir Julian Huxley and his brother, the novelist Aldous Huxley (the Huxley Institute was named in their honor), as well as the ailments, real and fancied, of Winston Churchill, Samuel Johnson, and other political and literary geniuses.

Osmond, who was a surgeon in the Royal Navy during World War II, knew a couple of Churchill's personal physicians. They always treated Churchill delicately and with a sense of humor because, Dr. Osmond recalls, "just one slip with a patient as mercurial as Winston Churchill could spell disaster."

Churchill suffered from depressions and various ailments much of his life, but he had the good sense to choose competent physicians who usually were witty, lighthearted, and optimistic in their style. Osmond recalls that one of Churchill's favorite physicians, Dr. Geoffrey Marshall, who had been one of Osmond's teachers in medical school, was "a brilliant, witty man who cheered Churchill greatly" with his amusing remarks while nursing Churchill through a bout of pneumonia in Marrakesh.

Osmond knew another of Churchill's doctors, Lord Moran, the chief medical officer on the Queen Mary. "Churchill developed an earache which Lord Moran did not see as being very serious. Churchill, suffering pain, did, so Moran scurried off to find Dr. G., a widely experienced ship's doctor used to difficult passages," Dr. Osmond recalls.

"Churchill was lying in his suite, flushed, irritable, and clearly in pain. He told Dr. G., 'Don't pull at my ear like that fool Moran, but give me something thoothing, doctor, thoothing.' Churchill had a slight lisp, which surfaced when he was stressed.

"Dr. G. produced some warmed almond oil and dropped it in gently. The results were magical. Churchill fell asleep and woke greatly refreshed. When the Queen Mary docked, he sent for Dr. G. and invited him to take a glass of sherry with him, saying, 'Doctor, I am much indebted to you.'

"Dr. G. said: 'No, Prime Minister, it is not you who are indebted to me, but I and all of us who are indebted to you.'

"Churchill put his hand on Dr. G.'s shoulder, tears came into his eyes, and he said, 'From the heart, doctor, from the heart. I am seldom spoken to from the heart now.' "

Dr. Osmond told me he is convinced "Jesus had an excellent sense of humor and pungent wit. If he hadn't, he could not have made such a favorable impression on publicans and sinners, and such an unfavorable impression on the religious establishment. The gospel brought glad tidings." But some have not always accepted the tidings gladly. Osmond observed, "You may recall Samuel Johnson's (Johnson suffered from recurrent depressions in his later years) remark: 'This merriment of parsons is mighty offensive!' "

In the late 1960s, I was greatly cheered by a couple of amusing letters I received from a then unknown psychologist named Dr. Laurence J. Peter, who was living in California. Dr. Peter became a member of the foundation, and we exchanged some entertaining letters. He told me of his theory that in any organization, one tends to rise to the level of one's incompetence, which he called "The Peter Principle."

Dr. Peter did funny things, like sending greeting cards to friends in mid-July, instead of at Christmas time. One card he sent on July 15 was in observance of "St. Swithun's Day." For almost twenty years, I thought St. Swithun was an invention of Peter's lively imagination. I did not discover until reading Butler that there actually was a St. Swithun. He was bishop of Winchester (A.D. 862), described by a contemporary as "a treasury of all virtues" and "attentive to the poor and sick." Many miraculous cures were said to be associated with his relics. His feast day is July 15.

This took place before Dr. Peter became a best-selling author with his book *The Peter Principle*, and his playful and gentle humor was a beam of light in the darkness of the psychiatric research jungle in which I was then entangled. It helped me hold on to my own balance.

The Wit as Doctor

Doctors, clergy, and other practitioners of the healing arts have been using humor as a healing tool for centuries. The famous Islamic physician Avicenna (980–1037) once was called to a home where he found a deeply depressed man huddled in a corner of the garden, mooing like a cow.

The man kept insisting that he was a cow and refused to leave the garden. Avicenna leaned over and ran his fingers along the man's thighs and hips. "Very well then," the physician said, "if you are indeed a cow, you are a very tender one and we shall have you for supper tonight."

He called for a butcher knife and went into the kitchen to find one. When he returned, the man was gone, and neighbors later reported that the man was cured from that moment.

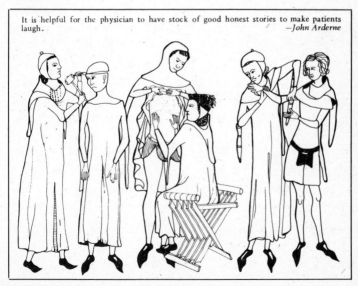

It is helpful for the physician to have stock of good honest stories to make patients laugh.
—*John Arderne*

Illustration courtesy of Institute for Cistercian Studies, Kalamazoo, Michigan.

A medieval professor of surgery, Andre de Mondeville (1260–1320) advised his students in his writings to "let the surgeon take care to regulate the whole regimen of the patient's life for joy and happiness." He urged doctors to "allow relatives and special friends to cheer up the patient by having someone tell him jokes." De Mondeville observed that "the body grows fat from joy and thin from sadness."

Robert Burton (1577–1640), the English parson and philosopher, observed that "mirth purges the blood, confirms health, causeth a fresh, pleasing and fine color, whets the wit, makes the body young, lively and fit for any kind of employment." Wrote Burton, "The merrier the heart, the longer the life." He described the three greatest doctors in history as "Dr. Quiet, Dr. Diet, and Dr. Merryman."

In medieval times, court jesters were esteemed as much as court physicians for their role in helping to preserve or to restore the physical and mental health of the king. Henry VIII kept around a court jester named Will Sommers, a Shakespearean comic actor. Sommers was described as "lean and stooped, yet to all the court, few men were more beloved than this fool . . . whose merry prate exiled sadness many a time."

In *Tom Sawyer*, Mark Twain wrote, "The old man laughed joyously and loud, shook up the details of his anatomy from head to foot, saying that such a laugh was money in a man's pocket because it cut down the doctor's bills like everything."

Another modern practitioner of humor in medicine is Dr. Douglas Lindsey, a professor of surgery at the University of Arizona in Tucson. Dr. Lindsey is a white-haired wit who has delivered papers at international conferences on humor. During the Korean War, Lindsey oversaw several M.A.S.H. Army units, one of which inspired the television series.

Lindsey, who works part-time in the emergency room at the University of Arizona Health Sciences Center, is an expert at putting a patient at ease with jokes or humor.

One day, a woman came into the emergency room and complained to one of Lindsey's medical students that she had a sharp pain in her buttocks and was terrified that she had cancer. Lindsey told the medical student to tell the woman that she had "proctalgia fugax" and he would come in later and explain the ailment to her.

The woman was overjoyed that she didn't have cancer and left before Lindsey had the time to explain to her that proctalgia fugax is Latin for "a fleeting pain in the hindquarters."

Father Jeffrey Keefe, a member of the Franciscan Order of Friars Minor, a clinical psychologist and professor of pastoral psychology at St. Anthony-on-Hudson, Rensselaer, New York, observes: "We are all turned off by pompous people. One reason is that pompous people lack humor. They are totally serious about themselves. The inability to laugh at oneself signals the lack of an essential human and humane quality. The humorless are likely to be proud while those who can laugh at self are honest enough to have a head start on humility."

Humor, says Keefe, can be a healthy strategy for letting off steam, and while it may be demeaning to poke fun at others, we might all benefit by poking fun at ourselves on occasion.

"Konrad Lorenz, an outstanding researcher on aggression, observes that barking dogs occasionally bite but laughing men hardly ever shoot," Keefe says. "Humor is a good way to tamp down the level of nastiness and violence in the world. We really ought to take humor more seriously."

Dr. Ladson Hinton, a San Francisco psychologist, has done pioneering work in clown therapy. Carmelite Sister Marie-Celeste of Reno, Nevada, who is familiar with Hinton's therapy, says that it is based on the idea that "our recognition and acceptance of the fool or clown that we really are puts us in touch with the truth about ourselves, stripping from ourselves the many masks we wear, the false pride and pretensions; at the same time it places a high value on the dignity of personhood."

In the otherwise bleak and solemn world of the mental health establishment, Dr. Walter E. "Buzz" O'Connell, a Jungian clinical psychologist at the VA Medical Center in Houston, Texas, stands out, along with Albert Ellis and Harold Greenwald, as a pioneer in the use of humor in psychotherapy. In his book *Super-Natural Highs*, O'Connell described how he uses jocular dismay and comic over and understatements to attack patients' feelings of discouragement and guilt. In O'Connell's view, the humorous attitude is the criterion of maturity.

O'Connell has been described by a couple of his colleagues as "an encourager" and "a lovable man with wit and healing on his lips." He routinely stamps his papers, books, and correspondence with the declaration: "STAMP OUT SERIOUSNESS." He once encouraged a student in his psychology class to write a paper based on the premise that "St. Peter was the archetypal screw-up."

O'Connell is one of the few psychologists to have done research on humor and healing.

"There are few source books for the curious to get an intellectual grip on the study of humor," says O'Connell. He plans to use this book as a text in his university-level psychology and religion class.

O'Connell noted that "professional interest in humor is

accelerating rapidly. International Congresses on Humor and Laughter have convened in recent years in Cardiff, Wales, Los Angeles, and Washington, D.C." Some psychologists and doctors are even beginning to study the physiology of humor. "Pain reduction and prevention of violence toward self and others through humor raise questions about the mutual interplay of endorphins, immunology, and humor," he said.

One theory suggests that laughter stimulates the brain to manufacture catecholamines, hormones that release natural pain-relieving substances called endorphins. Other doctors have observed that laughing also is good exercise for the lungs, heart, diaphragm, and stomach, and helps circulation by clearing toxins from the respiratory system.

Father Tom Walsh, a psychotherapist, has taught a popular course called "Humor, Hilarity, Healing, and Happy Hypothalami" at the Franciscan Renewal Center and churches in the Phoenix area. Walsh, who has counseled many depressed persons, observes, "You cannot be depressed, or anxious, or angry when you're laughing. It can't be done."

Someone once figured out that it takes seventy-two muscles to frown, and only fifteen to smile. "It's a lot of hard work to frown," Walsh says, "so why frown when smiling feels so good and is so easy?"

In 1981, Walsh wrote to about thirty persons in the helping professions—physicians, psychologists, social workers, counselors, and a couple of humorists—and asked them if they felt humor and laughter help the healing process. The responses were highly affirmative.

Mary Jane Belfie, a nun and psychologist in Lafayette, Louisiana, responded, "Whoever said, 'After Jesus, laughter is our best savior,' has me envious. I wish I had said it first. At least I am the one to say it most. Something special happens when people laugh together over something genuinely funny, and not hurtful to anyone. It's like a magic rain that showers down feelings of comfort, safety, and belonging to a group."

Dr. William S. Rutti, a Scottsdale dermatologist, responded, "While disease is not all psychosomatic, I feel that those that are can be influenced by our emotions. I find that humor can be useful to boost the spirits of patients."

Edward E. Ford, lecturer, consultant, and author of many books on relationships, including *Choosing to Love*, said, "I believe the good Lord created humor in us to help us make it through life. Laughter is a relaxant. The opposite of laughter is criticism. Criticism destroys relationships; laughter builds them."

Ford said he believes that "laughter is developed early in life through play. Unfortunately, because children are deprived of play through television watching, we are raising humorless children today. Laughter and humor are hard to find, especially in the media. That is why teaching is so dull in so many schools and universities. There is no humor."

Dr. John McBride, a Phoenix psychotherapist, responded, "Laughter is God's hand on the shoulder of a troubled world. This would be a bleak and dreary world without humor. The ability to laugh at ourselves is the next greatest gift we have to love. The cut-and-dried scientific approach to human life is one of the major catastrophes of today. When we take away the ability to laugh with chemicals, we destroy an important aspect of humankind. The first symptom of the emotionally ill person is his lack of laughter. I believe we have to celebrate life with laughter."

Mary Ann Wall, a Phoenix counselor, replied, "Personally and professionally, there's no doubt for me that humor is of great importance in the process of emotional healing and just managing daily stresses. In every one of my workshops, classes, retreats, I have found it very valuable to set some time aside for lighthearted, childlike playfulness. It is my contention that you can't stay depressed long if you are laughing.

"Unfortunately, I think counseling in the past has had a reputation of being so heavy that there is no place for laughter. Often, a client comes away more depressed, and so does the counselor."

Wall noted that the previous week she had been home sick with a cold, "and during our prayer-time, Bob [her husband] asked God to 'please heal Mary Ann so there will be more laughter again!' "

Truman Laughed Away His Mistakes

Another Scottsdale counselor, Father Paul Alvey, responded with this anecdote about President Harry Truman:

"Mr. President," a reporter asked Truman, "are you afraid of making mistakes?"

"No," Truman said. "If I were, I could never make a decision. I have to make a decision every day, and I know that fifty percent of them will be wrong. But then that leaves me fifty percent right, and that's batting five hundred."

"How do you handle the fifty percent wrong?" the reporter asked.

Truman replied, "I laugh at them, and at myself, and so does Bess."

Observed Alvey: "Too many people make their love of us contingent. If you don't make mistakes by their standards, they will love you. I think we need to know that we are lovable just as we are. Then we can laugh at ourselves and feel comfortable as others laugh with us."

Barry Brunsman, a Franciscan counselor in Caphoia, California, observed, "Humor is hope. Humor brings strength where there is weakness. Humor puts fun into the drama of sickness. Healing is accelerated."

Bil Keane, syndicated cartoonist and creator of "Family Circus," observed, "Humor can keep us healthy. It has kept all the Keane family healthy for three decades. Laughter is the safety valve of the mind. There is no better way to keep emotionally stable than by laughing or creating laughs."

Keane recalled that during World War II he was headed overseas on board a troopship in the South Pacific. The troops were bound for combat, and "the mental condition of most of the men was dismal, melancholy, and even despairing.

"I drew some big poster-size cartoons of the guys in this morose state and taped them around the ship. I poked unholy fun at our plight, the war, the food, the officers, and the ridiculous glum atmosphere. They resented it at first, but then realized that this commentary was coming from a guy in the same boat, and they laughed, not only at themselves, but with the realization that one of their own troops was lighthearted enough to puncture the gloom with potshots of sunshine and levity.

"Months later, the division chaplain told me how much he admired what I had done, reversing the low morale among the four thousand men aboard the ship.

"During the Vietnamese war, I toured throughout Vietnam with five other nationally known cartoonists who drew caricatures and performed little shows for U.S. personnel in outposts and hospitals. In one field hospital, I passed by the bed of a white-faced young soldier who had both legs missing and multiple chest wounds.

"The commander of the medical unit asked if I would do a drawing of this critically wounded fellow who was motionless and staring vacantly into space. I drew a quick cartoon and placed it in the patient's fingers. He slowly raised the drawing to eye level, a smile lighted his face, and he said, 'Thank you.'

"Later, the doctor told me, 'That's the first sign of emotion we've had out of that man since he's been here. I think now he's going to make it.' "

Keane added, "Laughter is not all 'ho, ho, ho' and 'ha, ha, ha.' It's also a quiet inner warmth that spreads good vibes throughout the mind and body. There is no doubt in my mind that laughter of any kind promotes better health."

Father Walsh, who years ago fought his own battle with a period of depression, says that he has observed healing begin in some patients when a clown visited a hospital.

A little girl, diagnosed as a catatonic schizophrenic in one children's hospital, sat in a rigid position for hours at a time, seemingly paralyzed with fear. She had been mute and totally unresponsive for six months. A clown walked through the ward, and the girl suddenly said, "Bo-Bo," her first word in six months. "That was the breakthrough in her case," Walsh said.

In another hospital, Walsh said, a ninety-five-year-old-man was suffering from depression. He hadn't spoken or eaten for days. A clown came into the ward, and in a half hour, the old man was talking and eating.

"How do you explain that?" Walsh asks. "I don't know. Who cares? But it works."

Marilyn Hood and her troupe of Sondancers from central Illinois use mime, song, dance, and narration to tell Christ-centered parables, and this extraordinary Christian clown ministry is in great demand at church retreat centers. When the Sondancers performed at John Michael Talbot's Secular Franciscan community, people laughed and wept and later described the parables as "healing experiences."

At a Jean Vanier retreat in Kansas City, the Sondancers enacted Vanier's ministry to mentally handicapped people through a parable, "Timothy: the Little Clown Who Helped the King's People to Laugh."

Another of the Sondancers' parables features "Theodore the Clown," who lives in a land where the king is missing from the throne. The message proclaims that the kingdom must be searched out and found within the heart in moments of self-giving. Love is the magic that helps one to see rainbows everywhere. The simple and the humble are the ones who find the kingdom. All who have seen the Sondancers agree.

Ever since he came across a painting of Jesus laughing a few years ago, Father Martin Clarke, a Franciscan Capuchin, has been using humor in his ministry as a chaplain at the Cabrini Medical Center in New York City. One day, Clarke was giving the homily at a noon mass in St. Patrick's Cathedral. He held a large picture, covered with a cloth, on the rail of the pulpit.

"For a minute or two," he suggested to the worshipers, "talk to Jesus within the depths of your heart." After a period of silence, the priest asked, "If you pictured Jesus in your meditation, what did his face look like? Was it the smiling face of Jesus with the little children? Was it the agonized face as Christ was being whipped by the soldiers? Or was it the weeping face of Jesus as he overlooked Jerusalem?" Then he added, "I will show you the face of my Jesus." He removed the cover from the picture, revealing a painting of a laughing Christ, and held it up to view.

A joyful hum rose from the audience, and the hundreds of worshipers burst into applause.

Clarke tells me he is now collecting paintings of smiling Christs, and has developed his own humor ministry.

Clarke picked up support for his humor ministry from Michael Farrell, columnist of the *National Catholic Reporter*. "Forget all those ponderous theories and explanations," Farrell wrote. "The main reason for all our trouble is that people have lost their sense of humor . . . The dark night of the soul is fine, but only masochists wallow in it . . . Every parish should have a humor committee."

At the University of Detroit, Jesuit Father Arthur Mc-Govern uses humor in his classroom and even teaches that humor can be brought into one's prayer life. "Overseriousness," he says, "can kill the meaning of life: Humor is a healthy corrective. We have to learn to laugh at our own failures and flaws. Otherwise, things get out of balance. Without a sense of humor, you focus on failures, defeats, lack of fulfillment. That leads to spiritual death."

McGovern says he sometimes brings humor into his prayer life. "We ought to present ourselves to God as we are," he says. "The relationship ought to be with God as it is with your closest friend. If you feel like joking with God, joke with him."

Helping Alcoholics with Humor

One weekend, our friend the late Bill Wilson, founder of Alcoholics Anonymous, invited us to hold a board of trustees meeting for the Huxley Institute at Guest House Sanitarium, a haven for alcoholic priests at Lake Orion, Michigan.

The sanitarium is located in a very luxurious mansion whose owner donated it for the purpose of helping alcoholic priests. The bar of one room has been converted into an altar where communion is served.

One night, Dr. Humphry Osmond gave a lecture on the

biochemistry of schizophrenia to an assembly of alcoholic priests and other AA members. Osmond was in top form, and while discussing a very serious and painful condition, he managed to include a barrage of jokes and one-liners that had the priests and all of us almost rolling in the aisles with laughter. The spirits of the priests were greatly improved after that evening. I was astonished at the spell that Osmond's wit seemed to cast over them.

Many years later, a couple of weeks before Christmas 1982, when I was still a single man, I attended a singles' discussion group at the Franciscan Renewal Center in Scottsdale. A mob of lonely people, ranging in ages from the twenties to the sixties, packed the room.

The discussion group was moderated by a warm and witty Franciscan priest named Gavin Griffith, an Irish leprechaun. Griffith ministers to both singles and alcoholics, and he is one of the church's foremost authorities on alcoholism. When an overworked friar or priest takes to the bottle, Griffith is often called upon to provide the emotional and spiritual support that he needs, and see that he gets medical care.

The singles loved Griffith. That night, he acknowledged that he himself is a recovering alcoholic, and he said he once heard alcoholism defined as "a Roman Catholic disease, recovery from which takes place in the basements of Protestant churches." He was just kidding, of course, but the crowd of Catholics and Protestants howled with delight.

Griffith handed out a mimeographed sheet listing some adult education courses that he would be offering that spring, and he invited people to sign up for them. The list included: "Overcoming Peace of Mind," "You and Your Birthmark," "Guilt Without Sex," "Whine Your Way to

Alienation," "How to Overcome Self-Doubt Through Pretense and Ostentation," "Christianity and the Art of RV Maintenance," "Exorcism and Acne," "Skate Yourself to Regularity," "Tap-dance Your Way to Social Ridicule," and "Bonsai Your Pet."

Some people, I later learned, actually signed up for the bogus courses.

The priest then sat down at a piano and led the group in singing some Christmas carols. When the singles returned home, they went with lifted spirits.

Griffith is a very devout and dedicated priest blessed with the gift of humor. He has taken the considerable pain that life has dealt him, and turned it—by some alchemy known only to God—into joy and humor that he shares with others.

Griffith is not the only clergyman who has reached and uplifted alcoholics with his sense of humor. Father Joseph Martin, another recovering alcoholic who has not drunk in twenty-six years, is cofounder of Ashley, Inc., a nonprofit treatment center for alcoholics in Havre de Grace, Maryland.

Martin also is in great demand as a lecturer on alcoholism. He is noted for his keen sense of humor and the vast repertoire of jokes he uses to illustrate his message that alcoholism is a "soul sickness" that can be conquered through Bill Wilson's Twelve Steps of Alcoholics Anonymous—and a sense of humor.

"A sure sign that an alcoholic is recovering is the return of a sense of humor," says Martin. "There is no humor in an alcoholic home. You can learn more and teach more through humor than by lecturing."

Martin says he has a good friend who, a few years ago, awoke one morning with a terrible hangover after drinking heavily the night before and saw a horse in his backyard. Curious, he went down to the kitchen and asked his wife what the horse was doing there. "You bought him last night and walked him home," she said. His friend has been sober ever since.

"There is one common denominator of the alcoholic: we are scared to death," observed Martin.

But humor can disarm fear. And doctors and clergymen are discovering that sometimes you can do most for patients simply by banishing their fears with a touch of humor.

The Humor of Charismatics and Spiritual Healers

It is said that the Devil cannot stand the sound of Jesus' name. It is also said that the Devil can't stand the sound of laughter.

Some preachers and evangelists have had the deserved reputation of being relentlessly gloomy, solemn, and foreboding. But lately, many preachers, evangelicals, charismatics, and Christian healers have been rediscovering the balancing and healing power of humor and are using it in their healing ministries.

They are rediscovering the meaning of the popular phrase "laugh it off" and learning that the Devil can be laughed off, too. People in the helping professions who are daily being confronted by persons in great emotional or physical pain need humor, as well as faith, to help them keep their own balance.

Some of the major names in the Christian healing and charismatic movements responded affirmatively to my article "Jesus Put on a Happy Face," in the September 1983 issue of *St. Anthony Messenger*. Clearly, if Christians can agree on little else, there is an almost unanimous ecumenical consensus that humor is healing.

Episcopalians Rev. Canon Alfred Price, Rev. Henry Getz and M'Lou Getz, and Rev. Rufus J. Womble report that they use humor in their healing ministries. Price, Getz, and Womble are past and present wardens of the Order of St. Luke, an interdenominational ministry of healing founded by Episcopalians. The Order of St. Luke conducts healing services in churches throughout the world.

Price, rector-emeritus of St. Stephen's Episcopal Church, Philadelphia, is a warmhearted, witty clergyman who, as international warden of the Order of St. Luke, has been a pioneer and pillar in the Christian healing movement for the past several decades.

"A Christian sense of humor is the finest of the fine arts," Price wrote me recently. "Morally considered, laughter is next to the Ten Commandments. We live in a world that is ravenously hungry for humor."

Price observed that "there is ample evidence to show that Jesus was not averse to laughter nor the comic incident in his teaching. In the New Testament, as in life, there are certain situations which can best be met by a flick of humor, perhaps met only in that way. Jesus knew when to use humor to its best advantage. A sense of humor saved Jesus from becoming discouraged with his slow and ignorant disciples.

"There is no cure for some of the evils of the world except perchance to laugh at them," Price said.

Price offered this prayer recently for the Order of St. Luke membership: "Our Heavenly Father, we thank Thee for a saving sense of humor. May we learn to smile through tears and to laugh in spite of sorrow and know that real humor is rooted in an unconquerable faith in the ultimate goodness of God. Help us to laugh at ourselves and not take ourselves too seriously."

Episcopalian healer Rev. Womble of Richmond, Virginia, who has been North American warden of the Order of St. Luke, wrote, "I agree with you that Jesus smiled a great deal. On a healing mission, I usually tell several jokes and then tell the congregation that God's healing love is working in them as they are laughing."

Dr. Ken Olson, a Lutheran pastor and clinical psychologist in Paradise Valley, Arizona, has treated depressed and anxious persons for many years. In private sessions Olson often uses humor to attack depression and anxiety. Olson, who directs the Center for Living in Phoenix, also frequently uses humor at the charismatic healing services he conducts in Lutheran churches in the Phoenix area.

"Laughter is such a marvelous tool to help us hang loose," says Olson, who is author of the best-selling book *The Art of Hanging Loose in an Uptight World*. "There is real healing power in laughter."

Francis MacNutt, director of Christian Healing Ministries, Inc., Clearwater, Florida, and the author of several best-selling books on the ministry of healing, wrote that he and his wife, Judith, a psychologist, use humor in their healing ministry.

Popular television evangelist, Father John P. Bertolucci, wrote that he has a picture of a laughing Christ on the wall at his Franciscan monastery at the University of Steubenville in Ohio. Bertolucci balances his gospel message deftly with a keen sense of humor and with funny anecdotes. He has the gift of channeling humor into the service of Christ.

The Catholic evangelist and healer Father Ralph DiOrio is also gifted in this direction. DiOrio is a humble and gentle man who feels deeply the pain of other people. "My personal pain bears no description, my pain literally breaks me, when healing does not seem to occur with the babies and little children," he said recently. "I honestly don't know why God chooses to heal some and not others. It remains a mystery."

But many people are healed through the prayers and touch of DiOrio. At charismatic gatherings, DiOrio's rich sense of humor emerges again and again. "You know," he said, pointing to a picture of a clown in his office, "I'm just like that clown over there. I'm a clown for God, carrying his love and his power and even sometimes his people for him." The humor helps to ease the pain—his own and those he is ministering to.

The charismatic movement has grown phenomenally in all denominations in the past two decades. An estimated twenty percent of all Catholics now consider themselves charismatics, and in the United States alone, between four and six thousand charismatic prayer groups meet regularly.

The charismatic movement is permeated with a spirit of joy, but a sense of humor, clowning, and laughter are not ordinarily listed by charismatics among "the gifts of the Spirit." If, as Jesus and Paul said, joy is a gift of the Spirit, the daughters of joy—humor, clowning, and laughter— also must be gifts of the Spirit.

Joy and Laughter Are Contagious

Depression and despair are contagious, but so are joy and laughter. In Syracuse, New York, Joan E. White has organized a club called "Joygerms," whose motto is "no dues, just do." What joygerms do is spread joy.

More than thirteen thousand people joined the club within a couple of years of its formation.

In Little Falls, Minnesota, where midwinter temperatures fall to forty degrees below zero, the nuns at St. Francis Christian Development Center have been sponsoring on February 2 a Laughter Day workshop to drive away the midwinter blues. Sister Monique, who calls February and March "crabapple season" because many folks are crabby, said the workshop focuses on the power of laughter to transform attitudes. Laughter is the theme of prayers, theological discussion, and faith reflection at the workshop.

Spiritual healing also can be the target of humor. This one came out not long ago: "Did you hear the Polish Pope's first miracle? He cured a ham."

That kind of humor has been around for a long time, and for a long time, clergy have been skilled in parrying insults with humorous retorts. Here's a classic example:

In the early 1800s, a minister with a doctor of divinity degree approached Peter Cartright, a rough-hewn Methodist minister, and asked him disdainfully, "How is it that you have no doctors of divinity in your denomination?"

"Our divinity is not sick and don't need doctoring," Cartright replied. (Years later, Cartright accepted a Methodist doctor of divinity degree without complaint.)

The nineteenth-century German philosopher Friedrich Nietzsche was acclaimed as a genius by many of his contemporaries. A melancholy and dyspeptic man with a colossal ego, Nietzsche is regarded as the spiritual father of many of the humorless secular tyrants, including Hitler, who have terrorized the twentieth century with war and bloodshed.

In his voluminous writings, Nietzsche attacked Christianity and the church with acerbic wit at every opportunity. Ironically, this proud, angry, and brilliant man spent the last years of his life in a lunatic asylum, helpless and babbling nonsense—in the care of a group of gentle nuns.

In his last years, Nietzsche had a glimpse of God, and also a glimpse of the Devil, who bore a striking resemblance to himself.

"I should only believe in a God that would know how to dance," he wrote. "And when I saw my devil, I found him serious, thorough, profound, solemn. He was the spirit of gravity—through him all things fall. Not by wrath but by laughter do we slay. Come, let us slay the spirit of gravity!"

But Nietzsche was no St. George. His dragon refused to be slain, and Nietzsche died a bitter, angry, sullen, terrified, insane man.

Many of the other proud, humorless, intellectual idols of recent centuries, like Karl Marx and Sigmund Freud, also went to their graves very sick, embittered, and mentally unbalanced men.

In his brilliant recent book, *Psychological Seduction, The Failure of Modern Psychology*, Dr. William Kirk Kilpatrick, a professor of psychology at Boston College, observes, "The hallmark of the psychological society seems to be an unremitting seriousness. The problem for us is that the serious tone of the therapist's office has crept into all the areas of our lives. Any ordinary remark we make seems to require analysis by our friends. The spirit of psychology is much like a calculating spirit. Where does this psychological seriousness come from? It comes from the attempt to take the place of God."

Kilpatrick adds, "The distinctive quality, the thing that literally sets paranoid people apart, is hyper-self-consciousness. In an excellent study of this sickness, David Shapiro observes, 'Paranoid people rarely laugh. They may act as if they are laughing, but they do not laugh genuinely; that is, they do not feel amused.' Why not? Because 'laughing always involves a certain degree of [self] abandonment. Playfulness disappears and playful interests are usually absent.'

"The point I have been at pains to make is that buoyancy is hard to come by in a psychological society. We are too weighted down by our own gravity, too freighted with self-calculation. And we do need to laugh—particularly at the state we have got ourselves in by taking psychology and ourselves so very seriously."

Jesus said there are many paths to self-destruction. I know, because I took many of them. There are many Pied Pipers of greed, hatred, and vengeance who will be eager to show you the way to hell.

If the Devil is always grave, solemn, and mirthless, one would suppose that it would be blasphemy to suggest that Jesus had the same qualities. Jean Leclercq, a Benedictine, asks, "How could Jesus have managed to attract children, women, simple people, if he was always aloof and serious?" He adds, "At a time in which anxiety forms the subject of so many publications . . . it is a good thing when the gospel of good humor, founded on detachment, is also preached."

The playwright Eugene Ionesco observed, "To become conscious of what is horrifying and to laugh at it is to become master of that which is horrifying . . . . The comic alone is capable of giving us the strength to bear the tragedy of existence."

That charming old wit George Bernard Shaw, who had a bit of the Devil in him and enjoyed poking fun at the church, nevertheless caught a glimpse of Jesus when he observed, "The older and greater church to which I belong is the church where the oftener you laugh the better, because by laughter only can you destroy evil without malice."

Humor thus is clearly a powerful healing tool (though it is only one healing tool), and the most effective healers I have known have had a keen sense of humor. If so many health professionals from so many different disciplines are using humor in their practices, surely Jesus Christ, the Great Physician, the greatest psychiatrist of all time, the healer of healers, must have used humor in his healing ministry. Surely Jesus used humor to calm the ill and disturbed, to allay their fears, to cheer up the mourners.

There is an old saying that "he who laughs last, laughs best." And who had the largest and most robust last laugh in history? The resurrected Jesus, who rose from the dead and laughed all the devils away.

In an Easter 1984 article for the *Boston Sunday Globe*, Harvey Cox, author of *The Feast of Fools*, observed, "In his *Divine Comedy*, Dante Alighieri reports that after he had made the tortuous ascent from hell to purgatory and then drawn close to the celestial sphere, he suddenly heard a sound he had never heard before." Stopping and listening, Dante wrote that "it sounded like the laughter of the universe."

The Easter story, says Cox, "gives us a clue to this baffling riddle" as to why God laughs. "God laughs, it seems, because God knows how it all turns out in the end," wrote Cox. "God's laughter is not that of One who can safely chortle, from a safe distance, at another's pain. It comes from One who has also felt the hunger pangs, the hurt of betrayal by friends, and the torturer's touch.

"Perhaps Easter Sunday provides us with the right occasion to reclaim the holy laughter that fell on Dante's astonished ears as his steps drew near God's dwelling place.

Chapter 3

FOOLS FOR CHRIST'S SAKE

In medieval Europe, a day called "the Feast of Fools" was celebrated, in which priests, monks, and laypeople painted their faces, put on comic masks, and cavorted all over town, singing absurd and satiric songs and poking fun at their superiors and various customs.

In France, it was called the Feast of Assinaria. The laypeople dressed up as "fool monks" and sometimes kidnapped the parish priest and made him "a fool bishop." It was an uproarious festival of clowning and good-natured teasing. Harvey Cox has described "the Feast of Fools" in a best-selling book by that name. The feast day was never popular with some of the church authorities, and the Council of Basel finally condemned it in 1451. But it went on for two hundred more years before dying out in the sixteenth century.

Here in the late twentieth century, the clowns are coming back to the church, and they're coming back in force. I am only one of thousands of Christians who have developed humor ministries in recent years. (My alter ego is "Brother Zorba," the unorthodox Greek Orthodox.) Many become "fools for Christ" and visit hospitals, nursing homes, and mental institutions to deliver hugs, jokes, and encouragment to the sick and the lonely.

The Missionary Servants of the Most Holy Trinity in Silver Spring, Maryland distribute a card bearing a laughing clown and this message from John Holmes: "There is no exercise better for the heart than reaching down and lifting people up." Martin Luther would have agreed, for he once said: "God is not a God of sadness, but the Devil is. Christ is a God of joy, and so the Scriptures often say that we should rejoice. . . . A Christian should and must be a cheerful person."

"Everyone has a clown inside," believes Carmelite Sister Marie-Celeste, of Carmel of Reno in Nevada, and author of a little gem of a book called *Clowns and Children of the World*. "Children let their clowns show, but after they grow up, most people have learned to hide their clown. Sometimes we even forget that they are there at all." She says her book is "a children's book written especially for grown-ups."

Sister Marie-Celeste neatly traces the history of clowning, beginning with primitive peoples who greatly esteemed their clowns and elevated them to the rank of medicine men. Among the tribes of Africa, among the Navajo Indians, and elsewhere, those who put on masks and costumes and helped people forget themselves and laugh at themselves often became the most important people in the tribe. Combining clowning with worship, they became medicine people who performed incantations and ritualisitc dances to drive away sickness. They served as cheerleaders for the tribe and taught young children how to survive. "They learned to make magnificent masks that exaggerated the emotions of people and would be easy for them to recognize: love and fear, hope and anger, happiness and hate," Sister Marie-Celeste observes. Thus, clowning was associated with healing even in primitive tribes.

In Europe in medieval times, kings became so powerful that they wouldn't listen to anyone except clowns. The kings brought clowns into their courts to entertain them with jokes, songs, dances, tricks, and magic. The king often would take advice from the court jester while rejecting the advice of the rich and the powerful. The court jester sometimes became the most influential political figure in the kingdom, able to get away with criticizing injustices, the court, and even the king.

Other clowns, Sister Marie-Celeste says, became wandering minstrels who traveled the country, usually with a pet dog and a musical instrument, and "sang songs to the people about what they ought to value as important in life." These clown-minstrels identified themselves with the poor and the oppressed. "They annoyed the authorities so much that laws were passed to silence them. But clowns are very creative, so they took to the stage."

Puritanism and the work ethic put an end to clowning and play. However, after the Industrial Revolution the clown reappeared in a major role with the traveling circus, and America fell in love with a procession of clowns like Dan Rice, Lou Jacobs, and Emmett Kelly.

The Return of the Christian Clowns

Only within the last two decades, however, has the Christian clown ministry been revived, and, interestingly, it is enjoying a parallel growth with the charismatic movement.

In 1986, many clergy and clowns of all denominations who had read the first edition of this book urged us to publish a newsletter that would focus on the joy and humor in Christian life and promote clown and humor ministries.

There was a clear ecumenical consensus among the thousands of people who wrote us, ranging from the conservative to the liberal, that good humor is good for your health.

There also was an ecumenical consensus that good humor is a peacemaking and bridge-building tool that can be used to defuse anger and hatred, reduce tensions, resolve conflicts, heal divisions among churches, and improve relationships in the home, workplace, school, and government. It is possible to wage peace with humor.

So in 1986, we organized the Fellowship of Merry Christians, a grass-roots ecumenical movement modestly seeking to recapture the spirit of joy, humor, unity, and healing power of the early Christians. The fellowship began publishing a newsletter, *The Joyful Noiseletter*, whose masthead carried a drawing of Jesus laughing. (Information about the Fellowship of Merry Christians or the newsletter may be obtained by writing to P.O. Box 668, Kalamazoo, Michigan 49005.)

We were overwhelmed by the response. In our first year, we enrolled over four thousand members from all denominations: clergy, hospital chaplains, nuns, doctors, psychologists, nurses, monks, humorists, comedians, authors, cartoonists, and clowns. Lots and lots of clowns.

We assembled an illustrious board of forty humorists as consulting editors to *The Joyful Noiseletter*, including cartoonist Bil Keane; Presbyterian theologian Conrad Hyers, author of *And God Created Laughter: the Bible as Divine Comedy*; healing minister Barbara Shlemon; Lutheran Chaplain David A. Buehler, who insists that "the shortest verse in the Bible is 'Jesus wept'"; Archbishop John L. May, the new president of the National Conference of Catholic Bishops who always ends his weekly column in *The St. Louis Review* with a joke; Baptist Pastor Tal D. Bonham, author of a series of *Treasury of Clean Joke Books*, Monsignor Arthur Tonne, a playful eighty-two-year-old priest who has written five volumes of *Jokes Priests Can Tell*; humorist Lois Donahue, author of *Dear Moses*; John Michael Talbot; Edward R. Walsh, an authority on Will Rogers; Terry Lindvall, who teaches a course entitled, "Humor and Satire in Communication" at CBN University; and Sondancer clown Marilyn Hood. All believe in developing strategies for humor as an aid to healing.

In 1987, the fellowship began cosponsoring "playshops" with church retreat centers to help persons gain a holy sense of humor. Participants are encouraged to take God more seriously and themselves less seriously.

Clowns played an important role in our first "playshop" at Alverna Retreat Center in Indianapolis, Indiana in the Spring of 1984. Marilyn Hood and her troupe of Sondancers charmed the retreatants with their repertoire of Christ-centered parables.

Another fellowship member who has an extraordinary clown ministry is Stephanie Whitcraft of Lancaster, Ohio, who hasn't allowed her own four-year battle with cancer to keep her from spreading joy and good cheer to others. Stephanie visits hospitals as "Heartwarmer the Clown," comforting, touching, and praying with patients. She also uses her artistic talents to design Heartwarmer bookmarks, postcards, stand-up placards, and other items with a variety of cartoon messages of love and humor.

"I taught elementary school before my illness," says Stephanie, who is still undergoing chemotherapy, "and God is allowing me to use the child-like things I've always enjoyed to keep me going now, and to help me teach others to cope—hopefully with a smile and the assurance of knowing a loving God. When forced by illness into a world of hurts and fears, I felt that God wanted me to touch people in a simple way."

In Olean, New York, David "Cupcake" McHenry has formed a group of Christian clowns "to bring the joy of our knowledge and faith in Jesus Christ" to the sick and lonely in nursing homes and hospitals.

In Corydon, Indiana, Keith Karnes, his wife, and their two sons have a clown ministry called "Karnes Klowns." "God has done great things through the clown ministry," says Keith. "We are convinced that clowns can reach people for Jesus when others cannot. People will listen to a clown."

Merry Christian Virginia N. Smith, aged seventy-eight, of Nashville, Tennessee, has for several years been dressing up in a colorful rooster costume she made and surprising retreatants at Emmaus Walk retreats. "It's great fun," Virginia says. "I dance the samba and the crowd goes wild when I remove the rooster head and they see my snow-white hair."

Bud and Lenore Frimoth of Portland, Oregon have been clowning for churches and street people for ten years. The married couple has also worked with the Commmpassionate Friends organization, which comforts people who have lost a family member. "Since we lost our own three-year-old child to cancer we are able to bring clowning [to the grieving parent] as a means of healing the gaping wounds of bereavement," Bud says.

One of the pioneers in the Christian clown ministry, the late Ken Feit, started out as a Jesuit and ended up as a traveling troubadour, mime, and clown, much loved by everyone he touched. A friend recalls, "Ken's heart was broken, even disillusioned by the events in America of the sixties. His passion grew out of compassion, and it drove him to—of all places—clown school to see if, in the midst of wars and rumors of wars, of institutional evil and social sin, he could learn some space, some humor, some transcendence. Here, in making contact with the spiritual tradition of the clown and later still with that of the fool and the storyteller, Ken would find his soul."

A Catholic, Feit was at home with everyone: Tibetan monks, Islamic sufis, or Native American shamans. "Ken Feit showed us the way to see through differences and barriers of ethnic, religious, racial, and economic divisions," the friend said.

"Ken loved the road the way a sailor loves the sea, knowing one day he would drown in it," another friend recalled. (Feit died in a traffic accident at the age of forty-one.)

Nick Weber, another pioneer in the Christian clown ministry, is a Jesuit priest who runs the world's smallest traveling circus: the Royal Lichtenstein & Quarter-Ring Sidewalk Circus. The Lichtenstein troupe, begun in 1971, performs for passersby at some 225 colleges, shopping centers, and parks every year. The group shares a low-key Christian message through clowns, jugglers, acrobats, dancers, magicians, and aerial acts, and mime fables.

Instead of lions and elephants, the circus's menagerie includes cats, birds, dogs, a horse, and a monkey.

Weber tells jokes, walks the tightrope, and eats fire, and he and his merry band try through play to rid their audiences of what they consider "a sterile, godless, and overcalculated life." Play, he says, can lead to prayer.

The circus is not a business; it is a ministry. "We aren't trying to make money," says Weber. "We're trying to get people to come together and play and recognize that they belong together."

Another pioneer in the clown ministry is Rev. Floyd Shaffer, a Lutheran pastor in Roseville, Michigan. Shaffer is a full-time clown in his role as Soccataco, and he has a large following. He and other Lutheran clowns sometimes serve communion dressed as clowns.

Pastors dressed as clowns serving communion appear to be a modern development. Not long ago, a couple of hundred clowns led by Rev. Shaffer participated in a communion service. Children and some adults have found such clown services delightful and moving. Other, more traditional, clergy and laity feel that the Eucharist is too sacred to clown about; that there is a time to worship and a time to clown; that there is a time to clown and a time not to clown; and that a gift that is appropriate and greatly needed in one setting may not be in another setting.

"The paradox of the clown appears in various ways throughout history," says Shaffer. "It seems to be an apocalyptic symbol that appears in times of hopelessness. Maybe clowns are raised at these moments in history as reminders that God is alive and well and continuing to work in the world."

Shaffer's alter ego, Soccataco, has observed, "The Christian Church has all the language of a party, but hasn't been able to pull it off."

The Sisters of St. Joseph of Nazareth in Kalamazoo, who sponsor a number of Catholic hospitals and nursing homes in Michigan, have a group of sister-clowns who visit the sick and the elderly. The organizer, Sister Mary Bader, a former president of Nazareth College, took her clown name "Fleur de Lis" because it is the name of the flower of France, the country of the order's roots.

This sister became a clown after reflecting on the meaning of Jesus' words in Matthew's Gospel: "I assure you, unless you change and become like little children, you will not enter the Kingdom of God."

Says Sister Mary, "Jesus wants us to come to him with the openness of a little child. Clowns are young at heart. They help us to look at our human weaknesses and aid us in bouncing up again and again.

"As Sisters of St. Joseph, we experience a certain sadness when we see suffering, unjustice, misery, in the lives of our brothers and sisters. We try to live in such a way that people can be reconciled with each other and with God, and then all that pain can be relieved. We are even willing to suffer so that can happen."

In circus tradition, she observes, the clown has the role of "a paramedic who is clowning around while watching for the needs of those who are performing dangerous routines. If there is an accident, the clown will distract you, take your mind away from the suffering and try to bring you joy."

She believes that "Jesus fulfilled the perfect description of the clown—one who takes pain to him or herself so that another may have joy. He came so that we may have joy that no one can take away from us. He laid down his life so that we might have life. Like Jesus, the clown takes on a different appearance—forgets who he or she is, so that others may know joy. The clown speaks to life, death, resurrection, to pain, joy, faith, hope, and love."

The clown, she says, laughs it up and pokes fun at the human frailties in all of us but does not ridicule or put down. "Real comedy brings down the high and the mighty and elevates the lowly. The clown has 'bounce-up-again' power to remind us to laugh at ourselves as well as with others, and at situations in which we find ourselves. The clown invites us to engage in the freedom of playful creativeness: the freedom of the children of God. The clown is a symbol of the resilience of our own human spirit, of the spirit of the daily conversion, starting over. A clown's mask can have a happy smile and teardrops telling us that there is going to be suffering and resurrection.

"How God must enjoy clowns!"

Sister Mary is a former retreat director at Nazareth Center in Kalamazoo, and the retreat center is laid out in a most unusual way. It has a "Hope Room," a "Rainbow Room," a "Desert Room," a "Seascape Room," a "Wilderness Room," a library, a chapel, and a "Joy Room."

The "Joy Room" is filled with paintings and statuettes of clowns surrounding a statue of St. Francis, the self-described holy fool who deserves to be the patron-saint of all clowns.

The Christ Clown

There are two kinds of fools identified in the Bible: the holy fools of God, and the unholy worldly fools who often are found mocking and even persecuting the fools of God.

Jesus was labeled a fool by Herod. And the Pharisees often claimed that Jesus was crazy, unbalanced, and possessed by demons. Before his crucifixion, Jesus was dressed in the robe of a fool, paraded through the streets of Jerusalem, mocked, and beaten.

Sister Marie-Celeste observes that April Fool's Day originally "was an early Christian feast celebrating the day [the Thursday-Friday preceding crucifixion] that Christ was dressed in the robe of a fool [a symbol of insanity], paraded through the streets, crowned with thorns, and mocked as an imposter king." This was thought at the time to have occurred the first week of April.

April Fool's Day was not just a day to play tricks on people. The early Christians saw it, she says, "as a sort of prophecy [of the road] that a Christian would have to travel in one way or another if he were true to his beliefs. It was the cost anyone would have to pay who set eternal values above the values of the world. April Fool's Day was a reparation made by the faithful to Jesus."

Sister Marie-Celeste has done an intriguing lithograph of Christ the Clown as "symbol of one who accepts pain to himself and returns only joy, love, and light."

"It began as a traditional face of Christ, as in Veronica's veil," she recalls, and ended in a rendering that "speaks of resurrection in terms of celebration, ticker tape, and circus symbolism, and places the Passion in relation to its fruit: the promise of eternal joy offered to humankind by one who paid the ultimate price, and invites participation by those who discover the clown in their hearts.

"Masks are like doors that cover our hearts. When we remove them, we leave our hearts open, and anybody and everybody is welcome to come right in. Just the way they really are. The thing that happens to clowns whose hearts are always open is that they get so full that they sometimes break. But if we keep them open, even then they mend. And they grow very large indeed: big enough, in fact, to carry the whole world, like a sobbing child, in their great love. Wouldn't you rather be a clown?"

In the clown book of etiquette, a cardinal principle is to "make others feel good." That is exactly what Dr. Morris B. Paynter and Lloyd B. Walton of Indianapolis, Indiana, have been doing for years with the Murat Clowns of Indianapolis.

Dr. Paynter is an eighty-three-year-old retired physician, but he is still a working clown. In 1972, he helped found the Murat Clowns, businessmen and professionals who donate their time visiting hospitals and attending parades throughout Indiana. Donations the group receives are given to the eighteen Shrine Hospitals for Crippled Children.

Says Dr. Paynter, "A good belly laugh is better medicine than any of the prescriptions they're dispensing now."

Walton became a clown after the death of his wife. "After she died, I retreated into an almost turtlelike shell and withdrew from all social activity," he recalls. That's when his alter ego, "Snap-O the Clown," was born.

"My greatest thrill," says Walton, "was when we were helping to entertain handicapped children. A seven-year-old clasped his frail arms around my leg. The love in his eyes made me gulp. The boy said, 'You're my special clown!' The interminable hours of studying clowning and applying makeup had paid off. I had made this child happy. And that's what clowning is all about."

The Murat Clowns like to repeat the Clown's Prayer:

Lord, as I stumble through this life, help me create more laughter than tears, dispense more happiness than gloom, spread more cheer than despair.

Never let me grow so big that I will fail to see the wonder in the eyes of a child, or the twinkle in the eyes of the aged.

Never let me forget that I am a clown, that my work is to cheer people up, make them happy, and make them laugh, make them forget momentarily all the unpleasant things in their lives.

Never let me acquire financial success to the point where I will discontinue calling upon my Creator in the hour of need, or acknowledging and thanking him in the hour of plenty.

And in my final moment, may I hear you whisper: When you made MY people smile, you made ME smile."

There is also a Fool's Prayer, written by Rev. Edward M. Hays:

Father and God of Fools,
     Lord of Clowns and Smiling Saints,
     I rejoice in this playful prayer
     that You are a God of laughter and of tears.

Blessed are You, for You have rooted within me
     the gifts of humor, lightheartedness, and mirth.

With jokes and comedy, You cause my heart to sing
    as laughter is made to flow out of me.
I am grateful that Your Son, Jesus,
    who was this world's master of wit,
    daily invites me to be a fool for Your sake,
    to embrace the madness
    of Your prophets, holy people and saints.

I delight in that holy madness
    which becomes the very medicine
    to heal the chaos of the cosmos
    since it calls each of us
    out of the hum-drumness of daily life
    into joy, adventure,
    and, most of all, into freedom.
I, who am so easily tempted to barter my freedom
    for tiny speckles of honor and power,
    am filled with gratitude that Your Son's very life
    has reminded me to value only love,
    the communion with other persons and with You,
    and to balance honor with humor.
With circus bands and organ grinders,
    with fools, clowns, court-jesters and comics,
    with high-spirited angels and saints,
    I too join the fun and foolishness of life,
    so that Your holy laughter
    may ring out to the edges of the universe.

There comes a time when even clowns must weep, and maybe even rage in anger at the injustices they see around them.

But the church and the world need clowns—plenty of them—and the fresh, joyful, vulnerable, but indomitable spirit they bring.

PART II

Centuries of Voices
Laughing in the Wilderness

Chapter 4

GOD LAUGHS
AND SO DO HIS PROPHETS

The Old Testament speaks often of weeping and wailing. But, if you look for it, there's also a lot of laughing and rejoicing going on, and God and some of the prophets are doing much of it.

One can identify two kinds of laughter in both the Old and New Testament. There is the laughter of the unrighteous and the doubting wicked, who are often found mocking or "laughing to scorn" God and the prophets. But God and the prophets, whatever hardships and persecutions they encounter, invariably have the last laugh. And the laughter of God and of the righteous is always spoken of in a positive way.

The word "laugh" appears for the first time in the Bible very early on, in Gen. 17:17. God informs the one-hundred-year-old Abraham that his ninety-year-old wife Sarah will give birth to a son. Recognizing a divine sense of humor, "Abraham bowed to the ground, and he laughed, thinking to himself, 'Is a child to be born to a man one hundred years old, and will Sarah have a child at the age of ninety?'"

God commanded Abraham to name his son "Isaac," which in Hebrew means "God's laugh." In Arabic, "ithaac" also means "he laughs."

There is something playful, even a bit teasing, about the way God approached Abraham and Sarah. "But Yahweh asked Abraham, 'Why did Sarah laugh and say, "Am I really going to have a child now that I am old?" Is anything too wonderful for Yahweh? At the same time next year, I shall visit you again and Sarah will have a son.' 'I did not laugh,' Sarah said, lying because she was afraid. But he replied, 'Oh yes, you did laugh' " (Gen. 18:13–15).

After she gave birth to Isaac, it was Sarah's turn to laugh. "Then Sarah said, 'God has given me cause to laugh; all those who hear of it will laugh with me' " (Gen. 21:6).

No doubt a lot of people did laugh, and laugh with joy—good, healthy, joyous laughter. And God, who clearly did not disapprove of their laughter, laughed with them. It is no small matter that in its very first book, the Bible establishes, very quickly, the image of a loving God who has a sense of humor and who laughs.

There are several references in the Old Testament to the laughter of the Lord. The Old Testament makes it very clear that God does laugh. For instance, the Psalms of David.

"Why this uproar among the nations? Why this impotent muttering of pagans? . . . The One whose throne is in heaven sits laughing, Yahweh derides them" (Ps. 2:4). "The wicked man plots against the virtuous, and grinds his teeth at him; but the Lord only laughs at the man, knowing his end is in sight" (Ps. 37:12–13).

In Proverbs, God declares, "Since I have called and you have refused me, since I have beckoned and no one has taken notice, since you have ignored all my advice and rejected all my warnings, I, for my part, will laugh at your distress . . ." (Prov. 1:24–26).

In the Book of Wisdom God says, "These people look on

and sneer, but the Lord will laugh at them. . . . He will tear them from their foundations" (Wis. 4:17–19).

Clergy of different denominations have found evidence of God's humor throughout the Bible. For instance, Rev. David A. Redding, pastor of Liberty Presbyterian Church in Delaware, Ohio, wrote a little book in 1977 called *Jesus Makes Me Laugh*. In it he observed that the story of Noah and the Ark "is rich with humor." I'm sure that comedian Bill Cosby, who did a classic piece on the Noah's Ark story, would be inclined to agree.

Redding also observed that "when God picked the political leader of the century to debate with Pharaoh, he chose a leader who was tongue-tied." Moses was the least eloquent of speakers.

Rev. Jim Lundeen of Gloria Dei Lutheran Church in Paradise Valley, Arizona, who occasionally dresses as a clown and plays the "Fool for Christ," is another pastor who is convinced that God has a sense of humor. "God has often given expression to his greatness and power in irrational, illogical, and even whimsical ways," observes Lundeen. "Like naming Gideon to go up against ten thousand armed warriors with three hundred recruits carrying as weapons a clay pot, a torch, and a horn; or selecting Amos, a fig picker, to go into the highest levels of government and preach social action sermons; or saving the world by sacrificing his Son on a criminal's cross."

Or making it possible for the aging and sterile Elizabeth to unnerve her crotchety husband, Zechariah, by giving birth to the infant John the Baptist. Or making it possible for a humble virgin to give birth to the savior of the world. Or sending the Messiah, the King of kings, the Savior of the world, riding on a donkey into Jerusalem, barefoot, penniless, and humbly robed.

Job's Friend Predicts He'll Laugh Again

One concordance lists fifty-seven references to laughter in the Old Testament. And there are also countless references to joy, gladness, rejoicing, and happiness. Where there are joy and gladness, rejoicing and happiness, you almost always find laughter.

The Preacher in Ecclesiastes declares, "There is an appointed time for everything, and a time for every affair under the heavens . . . a time to weep, and a time to laugh; a time to mourn, and a time to dance . . ." (3:1–4).

So there also must be a God who sometimes weeps and sometimes laughs.

"The patient man will hold out 'til the time comes, but his joy will break out in the end," according to Eccles. 1:23.

That was the experience of Job, a good servant of the Lord who couldn't understand why he was visited by disease, loss of wife and children, family, friends, and fortune. The book of Job is a chronicle of misery and sophisticated, self-pitying whining. "If only my misery could be weighed and all my ills be put on scales! But they outweigh the sands of the seas," Job, who has been reduced to skin and bones, laments (Job 6:1–3).

Job is in such a bad state of mind that the laughter of others is clearly annoying to him. "A man becomes a laughingstock to his friends if he cries to God and expects an answer," he cries out (Job 12:4). He can find no reason to laugh.

But two of Job's comforters assure him that he will one day laugh again. Bildad of Shuah tells Job, "Once again your cheeks will fill with laughter, from your lips will break a cry of joy!" (Job 8:21). And Eliphaz of Teman tells Job, "Happy indeed the man whom God corrects! . . . For he who wounds is he who soothes the sore, and the hand that hurts is the hand that heals . . . Six times he will deliver you from sorrow. You shall laugh at drought and frost . . ." (Job 5:17–22).

In his misery, Job does not believe them. But his friends Bildad and Eliphaz are prophetic. The Lord raises Job to laugh again.

But first, the Lord, obviously tiring of Job's whining, doubting, and endless questions, tells Job that although he loves him, Job is puny in the scheme of creation. God's final word reminds Job that it was not he but God, who created the brave horse who "laughs at fear; he is afraid of nothing" (Job 39:19–22), or who created the Leviathan who "laughs at the whirring javelin" (Job 41:21).

The brave, laughing horse and the fearless, laughing Leviathan are symbols of God's power. God, too, is fearless and laughs in the face of adversity. God is telling Job to stop whining and complaining and intellectualizing, and to get hold of himself and be like the horse and the Leviathan— brave and laughing in the face of adversity or combat.

Job suddenly stops doubting God and trying to justify himself. He admits his ignorance: "I have been holding forth on matters I do not understand" (Job 42:3). He repents "in dust and ashes."

God restores Job to good health and gives him a big family, friends, and more goods than he had before. And Job lives to the ripe old age of 140, a happy, contented man.

There is one very intriguing line at the end of Job's story: "Yahweh restored Job's fortunes because he had prayed for his friends" (Job 42:10). Is God telling us that when we pray for others, we unleash healing forces in ourselves?

Can you imagine the intensity of the joy of a man who has been raised from his personal hell and given so many blessings? I suspect that, like the laughing horse and the laughing Leviathan, Job laughed all the way through the rest of his long life.

God Delivers David from Recurrent Depressions

David clearly suffered from recurrent episodes of melancholia, followed by flights of ecstatic joy. In Psalm 86, the deeply depressed David pleads with his God: "Give joy to your servant, O Lord, for to you I lift up my soul."

David has problems. He is being pursued by an angry, vindictive, relentless King Saul. In Psalm 51 he prays to the Lord to "instill some joy and gladness into me, let the bones you have crushed rejoice again" (8–9).

The Lord was merciful to David and did give him the gift of joy he begged for. And David responded with thanksgiving:

"Sing joyfully to the Lord, all you lands; serve the Lord with gladness! Come before him with joyful song" (Ps. 100). "Let your faithful ones shout merrily for joy" (Ps. 132:9). "I am willing to act like a fool in order to show my joy in the Lord," says a joyful, dancing King David in 2 Sam. 7:21.

Many of the Old Testament prophets were continuously praying to the Lord not to turn his face away from them, and to grant the gift of joy. The prophets of the Old Testament knew what many modern doctors know: that a cheerful attitude of mind can help mobilize the body's defenses against disease.

The writer of Eccles. 11:9–10 advises, "Rejoice, O young man, while you are young, and let your heart be glad in the days of your youth . . . Ward off grief from your heart and put away trouble from your presence . . ."

"Do not abandon yourself to sorrow, do not torment yourself with brooding. Gladness of heart is life to a man, joy is what gives him length of days . . . Beguile your cares, console your heart, chase sorrow away; for sorrow has been the ruin of many, and is no use to anybody. Jealousy and anger shorten your days, and worry brings premature age . . . A genial heart makes a good trencherman, one who benefits from his food" (Eccles. 30:21–25). (Note: a trencherman is a person who has a hearty appetite.)

"You who fear the Lord hope for good things, for everlasting happiness and mercy" (Eccles. 2:9).

Solomon observed, "Happy the man who discovers wisdom, the man who gains discernment" (Prov. 3:13).

The writer of Proverbs found happiness in a wife who, among other virtues, could laugh. "A perfect wife—who can find her? She is far beyond the price of pearls . . . She is clothed in strength and dignity, she can *laugh* at the days to come . . . When she opens her mouth, she does so wisely; on her tongue is kindly instruction" (Prov. 31:10–25).

A wife like that will make a man cheerful. "Happy the husband of a really good wife; the number of his days will be doubled. A perfect wife is the joy of her husband; he will live out the years of his life in peace. A good wife is the best of portions, reserved for those who fear the Lord; rich or poor, they will be glad of heart, cheerful of face, whatever the season" (Eccles. 26:1–4).

The prophet Jeremiah laughed at the idols made by goldsmiths. "They are a Nothing, a laughable production" (Jer. 51:18).

Jeremiah delivered this message from the Lord, promising the return of the scattered Jews: "Thus says the Lord: 'See! I will restore the tents of Jacob, his dwellings I will pity; city shall be rebuilt upon hill, and palace restored as it was; from them will resound songs of praise, *the laughter of happy men'* " (Jer. 31:18–19).

Psalm 126, the song of returning exiles, declares,

When Yahweh brought Zion's captives home, at first it seemed like a dream;

Then our mouths filled with laughter and our lips with song.

Even the pagans started talking about the marvels Yahweh had done for us!

What marvels indeed he did for us, and how overjoyed we were! . . . Those who went sowing in tears now sing as they reap.

Daniel's Practical Joke on the Priests of Bel

Everyone knows that, when the prophet Daniel was thrown into the lion's den, the lions were reluctant to eat him. But my favorite story about Daniel—and, I think, the funniest story in the Bible—is how the prophet confounded the seventy priests of Bel and their many wives and children. The story fairly crackles with humor.

There was in Babylon an idol called Bel, to which twelve bushels of flour, forty sheep, and six measures of wine were offered every day. King Cyrus of Persia went to worship the idol every day. Cyrus asked Daniel, "Why do you not worship Bel?"

"I worship the living God who made heaven and earth and who has power over all living creatures," Daniel replied.

The king said, "You believe, then, that Bel is not a living God? Can you not see how much he eats every day?"

"Daniel laughed" (Dan. 14:7).

"My king," Daniel said, "do not be taken in; he is clay inside and bronze outside and has never eaten or drunk anything."

That made old King Cyrus angry. He summoned his priests and said, "Tell me who eats all this food, or die. Prove to me that Bel really eats it, and I will have Daniel put to death for blaspheming him."

The priests told the king to set out food and wine inside the temple of Bel, shut the door and seal it with his own seal. "If, when you return in the morning, you do not find that everything has been eaten by Bel, then let us be put to death; if not, then Daniel, the slanderer," the priests told the king.

The priests had a secret entrance to the temple, under the table, and every day they would enter the temple by this secret entrance and remove the food and wine. Daniel knew this, but the priests didn't know he knew it. When the priests had gone, Daniel told his servants to bring ashes and spread them all over the temple floor, with no other witness than the king. They then left the building and shut and sealed the door.

At night, as usual, the priests came to the temple with their wives and children and ate and drank everything. Early next morning, the king and Daniel went to the temple. The king broke the seal, opened the door and, seeing the food and wine gone, exclaimed: "You are great, O Bel! There is no deception in you."

"But Daniel laughed" (Dan. 14:19).

He told the king to look at the footprints of men, women, and children on the floor, and then showed him the secret door. The angry king ordered his priests arrested and handed Bel over to Daniel, who destroyed both the idol and the temple.

Daniel and his friends must have gone home and laughed their heads off.

In his book, *The Teacher*, Zvi Kolitz tells this story taken from the Talmud:

Rabbi Beroka used to visit the marketplace, where the Prophet Elijah often appeared to him. It was believed, as you know, that Elijah appeared to some saintly men to offer them spiritual guidance. Once Rabbi Beroka asked the prophet, "Is there anyone here who has a share in the world to come?"

"No," the prophet replied.

While they were talking, two men passed them by. On seeing them, the prophet remarked, "These two men have a share in the world to come."

Rabbi Beroka then approached and asked them, "Can you tell me what is your occupation?"

"We are jesters," they replied. "When we see men depressed, we cheer them up."

Back in 1968, Paulist Press published a fascinating book called *The Gift of Joy*. In one article, Pietro Dacquino wrote, "The joy of the Hebrews was therefore one which did not neglect the body but closely associated it with feasting and rejoicing by means of a 'good' meal, the 'garment of gladness,' and a drink of choice wine. Even music, harps and tambourines, song and dancing served to express and measure it."

Dacquino observed that, to the Hebrews, the reasons for feasting and rejoicing included the birth of children, the presence of the beloved spouse, longevity, prosperity, and abundance at the time of the vintage of the harvest, deliverance from enemies or victory over them, the coronation of the king, the presence of just leaders, and the peace of the nation.

Even a single glance of benevolence or a good work was sufficient to give joy. It shone through a radiant countenance. However, it is not a question of epicurean joy, as might appear to our modern mentality, but of a spontaneous and complete joy involving the whole man—body and spirit. So true is this that joy itself is regarded by the Hebrews as a gift of God (Eccles. 3:13) and is often linked up with religious feasts and liturgical worship . . . It was a joy entirely opposed to that false and materialistic joy of certain other contemporaries or to the orgiastic joy of the neighboring peoples. It was a gift of God, and when he wished to punish his unfaithful people, he would threaten precisely to take away all joy and exultation from their midst.

The joy of the Old Testament prefigures the advent of the joyful Messiah.

Chapter 5

THE JOYFUL CHRIST

In one of her delightful books, *At Wit's End*, Erma Bombeck tells this story:

In church the other Sunday, I was intent on a small child who was turning around smiling at everyone. He wasn't gurgling, spitting, humming, kicking, tearing the hymnals, or rummaging through his mother's handbag. He was just smiling.

Finally, his mother jerked him about and in a stage whisper that could be heard in a little theater off Broadway said: "Stop that grinning! You're in church!" With that, she gave him a belt and as the tears rolled down his cheeks added, "That's better," and returned to her prayers.

We sing, "Make a joyful noise unto the Lord!" while our faces reflect the sadness of one who has just buried a rich aunt who left everything to her pregnant hamster. We chant, "If I have not charity, I am become a sounding brass or a tinkling cymbal." Translated in the parking lot it comes out, "And the same to you, fella!"

Suddenly I was angry. It occurred to me the entire world is in tears, and if you're not, then you'd better get with it. I wanted to grab this child with the tear-stained face close to me and tell him about my God. The happy God. The smiling God. The God who had to have a sense of humor to have created the likes of us.

I wanted to tell him He is an understanding God. One who understands little children who pick their noses in church because they are bored. He understands the man in the parking lot who reads the comics while his wife is attending church. He even understands my shallow prayers that implore, "If you can't make me thin, then make my friends look fat." I wanted to tell him I've taken a few lumps in my time for daring to smile at religion. By tradition, one wears faith with the solemnity of a mourner, the gravity mask of tragedy, and the dedication of a Rotary badge.

What a fool, I thought. Here was a woman sitting next to the only thing left in our civilization—the only hope, our only miracle—our only promise of infinity. If he couldn't smile in church, where was there left to go?*

I love Erma Bombeck, and this is one of my favorite pieces by her. But she is only partly correct when she says there's a tradition of solemnity in Christianity. There is indeed a tradition of Christian solemnity coming down to us through the centuries. But there is also a parallel tradition of Christian merriment, wit, and high good humor.

In one New Testament concordance, there are 287 references to joy, gladness, merriment, rejoicing, delighting, laughing, etc.

Many passages from the Old Testament suggest that the people of Israel were not looking for a gloomy Messiah. They suggest, in fact, that the Messiah, when he came, would bring with him not only peace and healing and salvation, but joy as well.

The forerunner prophet, Isaiah, anticipated the advent of a joyful Messiah. "The spirit of the Lord God is upon me, because the Lord has anointed me; He has sent me to bring *glad tidings* to the lowly, to heal the broken-hearted . . . to give them the *oil of gladness* in place of mourning, a glorious

---

*Excerpt from *At Wit's End* by Erma Bombeck. Copyright © 1965, 1966, 1967 by Newsday, Inc. Reprinted by permission of Doubleday & Company, Inc.

mantle instead of a listless spirit" (Isa. 61:1–3). "I rejoice
heartily in the Lord, in my God is the joy of my soul" (Isa.
62:10). "Everlasting joy shall be theirs" (Isa. 67:2).

When he did appear, Jesus imparted a spirit of great joy,
as well as peace, to people—from his birth to shortly before
his crucifixion and after his resurrection.

A spirit of joy, exultation, rejoicing, and celebration surrounded the births of both John the Baptist and Jesus.
When the angel appeared to Zechariah and announced that
his aging wife Elizabeth would bear him a son whom he
must name John, the angel told him, "He will be your *joy*
and delight and many will rejoice at his birth, for he will be
great in the sight of the Lord" (Luke 1:14–15).

There was a spirit of joy when the angel Gabriel appeared to the Virgin Mary to announce that she would bear
a son named Jesus. The very first word Gabriel said was,
"Rejoice!" "Rejoice, highly favored daughter! The Lord is
with you!" (Luke 1:28). When the pregnant Mary went to
visit the pregnant Elizabeth, Elizabeth "gave a loud cry and
said, 'Of all women you are the most blessed, and blessed is
the fruit of your womb. Why should I be honored with a
visit from the mother of my Lord? For the moment your
greeting reached my ears, the child in my womb *leaped for
joy*' "(Luke 1:42–44). When Elizabeth gave birth to John
the Baptist, her neighbors and relatives "shared her *joy*"
(Luke 1:58).

When the angel appeared to the shepherds, the first
thing he said was, "Do not be afraid. Listen, I bring you
news of great *joy*, a *joy* to be shared by the whole people.
Today in the town of David a savior has been born to you;
he is Christ the Lord" (Luke 2:10–12). The magi were filled
with joy when they met the Christ child. "The sight of the
star filled them with delight, and going into the house they

saw the child with his mother Mary, and falling to their knees, they did him homage'' (Matt. 2:10).

This Was No Gloomy Messiah

Pietro Dacquino observes that ''the gospels, in speaking of the coming of Jesus, place such insistent emphasis on the joy and exultation that accompanied him. Luke, in particular, speaks repeatedly of joy. The gospel of John also mentions joy frequently.''

Jesus' first official act, notes Rev. Redding, was a miracle performed at a joyous celebration—a wedding—and he changed 120 gallons of water into wine for the party. A Messiah would have to have a sense of humor to start his ministry as a winemaker and bartender. The Pharisees must have been scandalized.

Jesus imparted a spirit of joy to his disciples and taught them to be joyful even in the face of adversity, tribulation, and affliction. ''Blessed are you when they insult you and persecute you and utter every kind of slander against you because of me; *be glad* and *rejoice*, for your reward is great in heaven'' (Matt. 5:11–12).

''To beatify'' means ''to make blissfully happy.'' A beatitude is a ''supreme blessedness; exalted happiness.'' The word ''blessed'' also can be translated as ''blissfully happy or contented.''

The Jerusalem Bible uses ''happy'' instead of ''blessed''' in its translation of the beatitudes of Jesus' Sermon on the Mount, ''happy'' and ''blessed'' being interchangeable.

How *happy* are the poor in spirit:
theirs is the kingdom of heaven.
Happy the gentle:
they shall have the earth for their heritage.

Happy those who mourn:
they shall be comforted.
Happy those who hunger and thirst for what is right:
they shall be satisfied.
Happy the merciful:
they shall have mercy shown them.
Happy the pure in heart:
they shall see God.
Happy the peacemakers:
they shall be called sons of God.
Happy those who are persecuted in the cause of right:
theirs is the kingdom of heaven.
Happy are you when people abuse you and persecute you and
speak all kinds of calumny against you on my account.
Rejoice and be *glad*, for your reward will be great in heaven;
this is how they persecuted the prophets before you (Matt. 5:3–
12).

Luke's account of the Sermon on the Mount includes:
"*Happy* are you who weep now; *you shall laugh. Happy* are
you when people hate you, drive you out, abuse you, denounce your name as criminal, on account of the Son of
Man. *Rejoice* when that day comes and *dance for joy*, then
your reward will be great in heaven. This was the way their
ancestors treated the prophets" (Luke 6:21–23).

I love the Sermon on the Mount whether it starts with
"blessed" or with "happy," but either way, I think it is clear
that Jesus' ministry is to bring joy and happiness into people's lives, not only in the hereafter but also in the here and
now.

These are not words of a gloomy Christ: "When you
fast, do not look dismal, like the hypocrites, for they disfig-
ure their faces that their fasting may be seen by men. Truly,
I say to you, they have their reward. But when you fast,
anoint your head and wash your face" (Matt. 6:16–17).

The disciples of John the Baptist asked Jesus, "Why do

we and the Pharisees fast, but your disciples do not fast?"
Jesus replied, "Can the wedding guests mourn as long as
the bridegroom is with them?" (Matt. 9:14–15). How can
one be sorrowful in the presence of the God of joy?

Again and again, in his parables and sermons, Jesus
spoke of joy, celebration, rejoicing, gladness.

"Tell me. Suppose a man has a hundred sheep and one
of them strays; will he not leave the ninety-nine on the hill-
side and go in search of the stray? I tell you solemnly, if he
finds it, it gives him more *joy* than do the ninety-nine that
did not stray at all" (Matt. 18:12–14).

A Joyful Father Embraces His Prodigal Son

In the parable of the prodigal son, Jesus spoke of the father seeing the boy while he was still a long way off. "He
ran to the boy, clasped him in his arms and kissed him ten-
derly" (Luke 15:1), and declared, " 'We are going to have a
feast, a *celebration*, because this son of mine was dead and
has come to life; he was lost and is found.' And they began
to *celebrate*" (Luke 15:23–24). Then Jesus reminded his audience that the father told his older, jealous son, "But it was
only right we should *celebrate* and *rejoice* because your
brother here was dead and has come to life; he was lost and
is found" (Luke 15:32).

The father ran to his prodigal son and embraced him
with tears of joy. And what did the father do? He didn't
judge him. He didn't lecture him. He didn't psychoanalyze
him. He didn't load him up with tranquilizers. He didn't
put him in group therapy. He didn't suggest a course in
mind control. He didn't exorcise demons from him. What
did he do? He threw a big party for his son, and they prob-
ably sang, circle-danced, and laughed away the night.

The great nineteenth-century Protestant preacher,

Dwight Lyman Moody, who often used humor in his sermons, expanded a bit on Jesus' story of the good Samaritan. "Suppose," Moody said, "a Methodist had been down there trying to get that poor fellow on his beast and wasn't quite strong enough to lift him up, and a Presbyterian had come along, and the Methodist says, 'Help me get him on the beast.' 'What are you going to do with him? What church is he going to join?' asks the Presbyterian. 'I haven't thought of that,' says the Methodist. 'I'm going to save him first.' 'I won't do it. I shan't help him till I know what church he is going to join.'

"An Episcopal brother comes along and wants to know if he has been confirmed. 'We haven't got time to talk about that,' says the good Samaritan. 'Let us save him.' 'What inn are you going to take him to?' asks another. 'A Congregationalist, Methodist, Baptist, or Episcopal inn?' "

Moody concluded: "Isn't that the spirit of the times?" Not much has changed through the years.

In the parable of the sower, Jesus spoke of the joy of those who receive the good news of the gospel but warned that they can also lose that joy. "Similarly, those who receive the seed on patches of rock are people who, when first they hear the word, welcome it at once with *joy*. But they have no root in them, they do not last; should some trial come, or some persecution on account of the word, they fall away at once" (Mark 4:16–18).

Are these the words of a gloomy Christ? "I have come so that they may have life, and have it to the full" (John 10:10).

Jesus transmitted a contagious spirit of joy to his disciples and to everyone he touched. "The seventy-two [apostles] came back *rejoicing*. 'Lord,' they said, 'even the devils submit to us when we use your name.' " Jesus responded,

"Yet do not *rejoice* that the spirits submit to you; *rejoice* rather that your names are written in heaven" (Luke 10:17, 20).

"It was then that, *filled with joy* by the Holy Spirit, Jesus said, 'I bless you, Father, Lord of heaven and earth, for hiding these things from the learned and the clever and revealing them to mere children' " (Luke 10:21).

"All the people were *overjoyed* at the wonders he worked" (Luke 13:17).

When Jesus saw Zacchaeus, the rich tax collector, in a sycamore tree, he called him to hurry down so that he could stay at his house. "And he [Zacchaeus] hurried down and welcomed him *joyfully*" (Luke 19:6).

When Jesus entered Jerusalem on a donkey, "the whole group of disciples *joyfully* began to praise God at the top of their voices for all the miracles they had seen" (Luke 19:37).

"Stop Crying," Jesus Told the Mourners

There are a number of passages in the New Testament indicating that Jesus' detractors and enemies mocked and *laughed at* him, both to his face and behind his back. King Herod called him a fool. Luke, relating the story of Jesus' cure of Jairus' twelve-year-old daughter, says that when Jesus arrived at the home, he found everyone weeping and mourning inside.

"Stop crying; she is not dead, but asleep," Jesus told the relatives. "But they laughed at him, knowing she was dead" (Luke 8:52–53). Jesus commanded them to leave and went in and healed the girl.

Jesus never laughed at an ill or hurting person. But it is not improbable that he prayed for this sick little girl, took

her in his arms, hugged and kissed her, and, when she came
to consciousness, perhaps even told her a funny little story
to relax and calm her.

Not everyone has the wisdom to discern when humor
can be healing and when it can be damaging. If not all food
is good for the stomach, not all humor is necessarily good
for the soul. But I believe the humor of Jesus Christ was a
healthy, healing kind of humor that lifted up people who
were down and deflated people who thought they were
above everybody else.

A lot of the passages in the Gospels crackle with ironic
wit, especially when Jesus is needling the Pharisees,
scribes, and lawyers. A skillful cartoonist could have drawn
on some of Jesus' remarks to fashion a set of delightful
cartoons.

For instance: "Beware of practicing your piety before
men in order to be seen by them . . . Thus, when you give
alms, sound no trumpet before you, as the hypocrites do in
the synagogues and in the streets, that they may be praised
by men" (Matt. 6:1–2).

Picture this cartoon: Preceded by a large band with
trumpets, trombones, and drums, a proud, well-dressed
man marches down the street, throwing coins to the poor,
while on the sidelines the well-fed applaud his generosity.

Again, this is the stuff from which cartoons are made:
"Woe to you, scribes and Pharisees, hypocrites! . . . You
blind guides, straining out a gnat and swallowing a camel!"
(Matt. 23:23–24).

"Woe to you, scribes and Pharisees, hypocrites! For you
traverse sea and land to make a single proselyte, and when
he becomes a proselyte, you make him twice as much a
child of hell as yourselves" (Matt. 23:15).

"Truly I say unto you, the tax collectors and the harlots go into the Kingdom of God before you" (Matt. 21:31).

I suspect that the large crowds following Jesus laughed heartily at his wit. It is no wonder that the authorities wanted to kill him. Pride and arrogance cannot stand to be deflated by laughter.

At the Last Supper, before his betrayal and crucifixion, Jesus again spoke of joy: "If you keep my commandments, you will remain in my love, just as I have kept my Father's commandments and remain in his love. I have told you this so that my own *joy* may be in you and your *joy* be complete" (John 15:11–12).

"I tell you most solemnly, you will be weeping and wailing while the world will rejoice; you will be sorrowful, but your sorrow will turn to *joy* . . . You are sad now, but I shall see you again, and your hearts will be full of *joy*, and that *joy* no one shall take from you" (John 16:20–22).

"Ask and you will receive, and so your *joy* will be complete" (John 16:24).

"But now I am coming to you and while still in the world I say these things to share my *joy* with them to the full" (John 17:13).

It is a paradox that Jesus would be speaking so often of joy on the very eve of his crucifixion.

A great sorrow descended upon the disciples before and after the crucifixion. But at news of the resurrection, the sorrow quickly changed into a tidal wave of joy.

When Mary Magdalene and the other Mary came to visit the tomb, an angel appeared to them and told them that Jesus had risen from the dead. "Filled with awe and great *joy*, the women came quickly away from the tomb and ran to tell the disciples" (Matt. 28:8).

When the risen Jesus appeared to the apostles, he immediately chided them for being "so agitated" and doubtful and invited them to touch him. "Their *joy* was so great that they still could not believe it, and they stood there dumbfounded" (Luke 24:40–41).

John, like Luke, also reports the intensity of the disciples' joy when the risen Jesus came to them and showed them his wounded hands and side. "The disciples were filled with *joy* when they saw the Lord, and he said to them again, 'Peace be with you' " (John 20:21).

After Jesus ascended to heaven, the apostles "worshiped him and then went back to Jerusalem *full of joy;* and they were continually in the Temple praising God" (Luke 24:52).

Our Sunday Visitor Publisher, Father Vincent J. Giese, went to Central America in 1984 to report on Catholic Relief Services' aid to the estimated two million refugees and displaced people in that troubled war-torn area.

Father Giese was invited to a mass for refugees at a chapel in Heredia, Costa Rica. "It was a moving experience to be part of this mass and a dialogue homily, as these strong people of faith, mostly women and children, stood up to comment on the Scriptures," Giese recalls. "The theme was love and peace, based on a reading from St. Paul. Father Higenio Alas, a dynamic man who is the father image to all the refugees, asked a little girl to comment on the Scriptures.

" 'Who is God?' he inquired, and everyone was sure she would reply, 'God is Love,' because that was the theme of the mass. Instead, she surprised the congregation by saying, 'God is joy.'

" 'A profound insight,' Father Alas said. 'We must penetrate its meaning.'

"The seven-year-old girl continued, 'Jesus was close to his disciples because they were his friends. When friends come together, especially to serve others, there is always great joy. So, God is joy. It is the same today.'

" 'But what about Jesus on the cross?' Father Alas asked her.

" 'Oh yes, he had perfect joy then, because at that moment he was giving everything he was and had to those he loved. He had to be very happy at that moment.'

"From the mouths of babes comes true wisdom."

Chapter 6

THE HAPPY APOSTLES

Mental health experts estimate that anywhere from thirty to fifty million Americans suffer from depressions of various intensities and durations. This is so in the midst of all the luxuries, creature comforts, material goodies, and freedoms that modern society provides.

In a world where depression has become an increasingly common ailment, it might be cheering to remind ourselves on occasion what many of us have forgotten and others do not know: that the theme of joy and merriment (as in "Merry Christmas" and "Happy Easter") runs recurrently through Christian history. Christians of all traditions expressed joy through the cruelest persecutions, from first-century Rome, where Christian martyrs went to their deaths singing hymns of joy, to the modern Soviet Union, where a young Russian Orthodox woman, imprisoned for her church activities, "goes to the punishment cell smiling and returns smiling."

The early Christians were widely known for their spirit of joy in the face of adversity and persecution. The apostles inherited the torch of joy that Jesus passed on to them, and every one of the apostles spoke repeatedly of joy.

Paul: A Cheerful "Fool for Christ"

A traditional Eastern Orthodox icon of Paul represents him with a rather sorrowful, sickly face. Paul's health, in fact, appears to have been somewhat fragile, and he often spoke of his "thorn in the flesh," which he prayed to the Lord three times to remove, in vain. His letters indicate that he also suffered, on occasion, from depression, anxiety, and inner turmoil.

And yet, the great mystery of Paul is that, while he was unable to heal his own "thorn in the flesh," God used him as an instrument to heal others, and he healed many of the sick, in the name of Jesus, with a word or a touch.

Paul had a long and hard Christian pilgrimage. The Lord made it clear to the disciple Ananias, who was sent to heal Paul and restore his lost sight after his conversion on the road to Damascus, that "I myself will show him how much he himself must suffer for my name" (Acts 9:16).

For fifteen years after his conversion, Paul was a homeless wanderer, rejected by his own beloved people, and distrusted by the many Christians he had persecuted but now loved. He said that no Christian ever taught him the gospel, but he received it through revelation. For fifteen years he retired to the deserts of Arabia and Syria, and possibly he preached to the pagans there, apparently with little success in terms of converts and churches. The Pharisees of Damascus and an official of the Nabatean king plotted to kill him, but he escaped with his life when his disciples lowered him in a basket through a window in the city wall (Acts 9:23). It is a comic scene, smacking of Charlie Chaplin—the underdog, pursued by the Keystone Cops, escaping in a bizarre way to live to drive his detractors crazy another day.

He went to Antioch, a thriving city of a half million people, the capital of Syria, the third largest city in the Roman Empire, the city where Jesus' followers were first called Christians, among other names. But again he was met by a storm of controversy. He was endlessly at odds with the pagan Greeks and Romans, the Pharisees, the newly Christianized Jews, and his own converts among the pagans. Yet, when Paul and Barnabas were expelled from Antioch, they "shook the dust from their feet in defiance and went off to Iconium; but the disciples were *filled with joy* and the Holy Spirit" (Acts 13:52).

A crisis arose among the early Christians over the issue of circumcision. Many of the Jewish Christians of the church in Jerusalem wanted to require the Christians of pagan origin, whom Paul had evangelized, to follow the Mosaic law of circumcision. Paul argued in his letter to the Galatians that imposing the Mosaic law on pagans as a condition for their conversion would hold up the progress of the gospel.

The issue threatened the unity of the early church. So what did Paul do? With a great sense of comic irony, Paul went to the apostolic assembly in Jerusalem in A.D. 48 and took with him his friend Titus, a newly converted uncircumcised Greek Christian. The Jewish Christians immediately demanded that Paul have Titus circumcised. Paul refused (Gal. 2:5) and finally convinced the assembly that he had been called to preach the good news to the uncircumcised. One can almost hear Titus's sigh of relief when the shouts for his circumcision died down.

Paul returned happily to his Greek churches, only to discover that the new Christians were quarreling and fighting among themselves, too. The Greeks were highly individualistic and boasted of their knowledge and philosophy.

They loved to argue and debate. "The Greek introduced, even into the religious domain, his exaggerated personalism and a limitless confidence in his natural intelligence," observes Father Lucien Cerfaux, another authority on Paul.

The church at Corinth was especially troublesome and broke into open rebellion against Paul. Itinerant preachers, pompous and windy, were challenging Paul's authority and counsel and reviling him. Paul contrasted his own humility and poverty with the learned arrogance and greed of these preachers, and he told them that the power of Christ is made perfect in the weakness of his apostles. "Here we are, fools for the sake of Christ while you are the learned men in Christ" (1 Cor. 4:10). "At least we do not go around offering the word of God for sale, as many other people do" (2 Cor. 2:17).

Worship services had become disorderly and tumultuous. Cliques and rivalries based on spiritual gifts had formed, and some people were taking an inordinate pride in their charismatic gifts, especially the gift of speaking with tongues. Paul recognized all these gifts as legitimate expressions of the Holy Spirit and did not try to squelch them. "I thank God that I have a greater gift of tongues than all of you, but when I am in the presence of the community, I would rather say five words that mean something than ten thousand words in a tongue" (1 Cor. 14:19). "And so, my dear brothers, by all means be ambitious to prophesy, do not suppress the gift of tongues, but let everything be done with propriety and in order" (1 Cor. 14:39–40).

Those Troublesome Greeks

Hounded by troubles and problems on all sides, Paul nevertheless doggedly reflected a joyful spirit in his epistles to the rebellious Corinthians. "We are in difficulties on all sides, but never despair; we have been persecuted, but never deserted; knocked down, but never killed . . . " (2 Cor. 4:8–9).

He began his letter to the Corinthians by advising them to bear their sufferings patiently and told them that he was working for their happiness. "We are not dictators over your faith, but are fellow workers with you for your *happiness*" (2 Cor. 1:24). "I could never be *happy* unless you were" (2 Cor. 2:3). "We are thought most miserable, and yet we are *always rejoicing*" (2 Cor. 6:10). "I am filled with consolation and my *joy* is overflowing" (2 Cor. 7:4). Comforted by the arrival of Titus, Paul remarked: "And so I am *happier* now than I was before" (2 Cor. 7:7). "I am *happy* now, not because I made you suffer, but because your suffering led to repentance" (2 Cor. 7:9). "With this encouragement, too, we had the even greater *happiness* of finding Titus so *happy*" (2 Cor. 7:13). "I am very *happy* knowing that I can rely on you so completely" (2 Cor. 7:16).

Paul praised the churches in Macedonia as examples of cheerful and generous givers. "Throughout great trials by suffering, their *constant cheerfulness* and their intense poverty have overflowed in a wealth of generosity" (2 Cor. 8:2). Paul concluded the letter to the Corinthians saying, "In the meantime, brothers, we wish you *happiness*" (2 Cor. 13:11).

Writing to the church at Rome in an effort to ease tensions between Jewish converts and non-Jewish converts, Paul wrote, "If you hope, this will make you *cheerful*" (Rom. 12:12). "*Rejoice* with those who *rejoice*, and be sad with those in sorrow" (Rom. 12:15). "The Kingdom of God . . . means righteousness and peace and *joy* brought by the Holy Spirit" (Rom. 14:17–18). "May the God of hope bring you such *joy* and peace in your faith that the power of the Holy Spirit will remove all bounds to hope" (Rom. 15:13).

He concluded the letter with an expression of his own happiness. "If God wills, I shall be feeling *very happy* when I come to enjoy a period of rest among you" (Rom. 15:32). "Your fidelity to Christ, anyway, is famous everywhere, and that makes me *very happy* about you" (Rom. 16:19).

Surely it must say something about Paul's character that he put "joy" second only to "love" on his list of fruits of the Holy Spirit. "What the Spirit brings is very different: Love, *joy*, peace, patience, kindness, goodness, trustfulness, gentleness, and self-control" (Gal. 5:22–23).

Paul's letters to the Ephesians and to the Philippians, written while he was under arrest, also are full of references to joy and rejoicing. Outsiders are supposed to cheer up prisoners; but here is Paul, a prisoner, trying to cheer up people outside of prison.

Writing from a prison in Rome, Paul advised the Ephesians to "sing the words and tunes of the psalms and hymns when you are together, and go on singing and chanting and everywhere you are giving thanks to God who is our Father in the name of our Lord Jesus Christ" (Eph. 5:19–20).

"Put God's armor on so as to be able to resist the devil's tactics" (Eph. 6:10–12). And the armor of God includes a spirit of joy, a cheerful heart, humor and laughter. The world, Paul knew, is full of deceivers, conmen, and peddlers of camel dung; and a holy sense of humor is a shield that repels the camel dung the world throws at you.

Under arrest in Ephesus, Paul spoke of joy at the very start of his letter to the Philippians: "I thank my God whenever I think of you; and every time I pray for all of you, I pray with *joy*" (Phil. 1:3–4). "Christ is proclaimed;

and that makes me *happy;* and I shall continue to be *happy,* because I know this will help to save me" (Phil. 1:18–19). "I shall survive and stay with you all, and help you progress in the faith and even increase your *joy* in it" (Phil. 1:25).

"Be united in your convictions and united in your love, with a common purpose and a common mind. That is the one thing which would make me *completely happy*" (Phil. 2:2). "And then, if my blood has to be shed as part of your own sacrifice and offering—which is your faith—I shall still be *happy* and *rejoice* with all of you, and you must be just as *happy* and *rejoice* with me" (Phil. 17:18). "Finally, my brothers, *rejoice* in the Lord" (Phil. 3:1). "I miss you very much, my dear friends; you are my *joy* and my crown" (Phil. 4:1).

His final advice to the Philippians: "I want you to be *happy,* always *happy* in the Lord; I repeat, what I want is your *happiness*" (Phil. 4:4). Another translation is: "Rejoice in the Lord always. I say it again. Rejoice!" "It is a great *joy* to me, in the Lord, that at last you have shown some concern for me again" (Phil. 4:10).

Under arrest in Rome, Paul wrote a letter to the Colossians which also begins with the exhortation that they endure all things joyfully. "You will have in you the strength, based on his power, never to give in, but to bear anything *joyfully,* thanking the Father who has made it possible for you to join the saints and with them to inherit the light" (Col. 11:12). "It makes me *happy* to suffer for you, as I am suffering now" (Col. 1:24).

Again, Paul began his first letter to the church of the Thessalonians speaking of *"the joy of the Holy Spirit."* "And you observed the sort of life we lived when we were with you, which was for your instruction, *and you were led to become imitators of us, and of the Lord;* and it was with *the joy of the Holy Spirit* that you took to the Gospel, in spite of the great opposition all around you" (1 Thess. 1:6).

This passage is a strong biblical confirmation of the joyous spirit of Jesus Christ and of his Apostle Paul. Paul declared in unmistakably clear language that the Thessalonians were inspired to imitate himself and the Lord Jesus in "the joy of the Holy Spirit."

If Jesus and Paul were gloomy and perpetually sorrowful, how could the Thessalonians imitate them in "the joy of the Holy Spirit"? In fact, the Thessalonians were striving in their daily lives to imitate a joyful Christ, and the apostle Paul, too, was struggling to be a model of joy, worthy of his Lord.

"What do you think is our pride and *joy*?" Paul asked the Thessalonians. "You are; and you will be the crown of which we shall be proudest in the presence of our Lord Jesus when he comes; you are our pride and our *joy*" (1 Thess. 2:19–20). "How can we thank God enough for you, for all the *joy* we feel before our God on your account?" (1 Thess. 3:9). Paul concluded the first letter to the Thessalonians with the advice: "*Be happy at all times*; pray constantly" (1 Thess. 5:16).

In the twilight of his life and while he was a prisoner in Rome awaiting death, Paul writes to Timothy: "I have fought the good fight to the end; I have run the race to the finish; I have kept the faith" (2 Tim. 4:7). Yet, again he spoke of his happiness at the top of the letter. "I remember you in my prayers; I remember your tears, and long to see you again to complete my *happiness*" (2 Tim. 1:3).

In a letter to a Jewish-Christian community, Paul again began with a reference to gladness. "This is why God, your God, has anointed you with the *oil of gladness*, above all your rivals" (Heb. 1:9).

"Let us not lose sight of Jesus, who leads us in our faith and brings it to perfection; for the sake of the *joy* which was still in the future, he endured the cross . . . " (Heb. 12:2).

So *it is that five of Paul's letters—to the Corinthians, Philippians, Thessalonians, Timothy and Hebrews—begin with references to joy, gladness, and happiness.*

These are the letters of a sullen saint?

The Boy Who Fell Asleep During Paul's Sermon

My favorite story about Paul, which shows his tenderness and humanity, happened in Troas when a boy fell asleep during one of Paul's endless sermons. Henry Ward Beecher, a great nineteenth-century Congregationalist preacher and wit, once remarked that the role of humor in church was to keep parishioners awake on Sunday. But even Paul's wit and eloquence could not keep this young man awake.

Paul "preached a sermon that went on 'til the middle of the night. A number of lamps were lit in the upstairs room where we were assembled, and as Paul went on and on, a young man called Eutychus who was sitting on the window sill grew drowsy and was overcome by sleep and fell to the ground three floors below. He was picked up dead. Paul went down and stooped to clasp the boy to him. 'There is no need to worry,' he said, 'there is still life in him.' Then he went back upstairs where he broke bread and ate and carried on talking till he left at daybreak. They took the boy away alive, and were greatly encouraged" (Acts 20:7–12).

Everything that Paul did encouraged people. He was a master of exhortation. He was the great encourager, the holy cheerleader. Here was a gentle and joyful man. In some ways, Paul reminds me of Charlie Chaplin's little tramp, who keeps falling, getting up, brushing himself off, and carrying on with a smile on his face. Paul was a model of cheerfulness in the face of adversity. Like the "fool for Christ" he later described himself (1 Cor. 4:10), he kept bouncing back from disaster with a defiant smile on his face.

Notwithstanding his many trials, tribulations, persecutions, imprisonments, thorns in the flesh, ailments, defeats, and depressions, Paul happily snatched the torch of joy that Jesus handed to him and ran with it. An authority on Paul, Prof. Francois Amiot of the Seminaire de Saint Sulpice observed, "Gratitude for God's blessings gives rise to a supernatural joy which persists even in the midst of suffering. Here again, St. Paul is our example. He is overflowing with joy, he says, despite all his troubles (2 Cor. 7:4), and he expects a similar joy to characterize all the faithful."

In Col. 1:15, Paul says of Christ, "He is the image of the unseen God, and the first-born of all creation." Paul saw that image as an image of joy, and he tried to emulate it.

Peter: The Slippery "Rock"

Peter was perhaps the most volatile of Jesus' disciples. He was an emotional man with a big heart, not noted for his stability. Jesus had to have had a sense of humor to name Simon Peter "Rock," and the other disciples must have laughed among themselves when Jesus announced that he would build his church on this slippery "Rock." Jesus gave "the keys to the Kingdom" to the disciple who tried to walk on water but panicked, fell in, and shouted to Jesus for help. What is this? A fisherman who couldn't even swim? When Jesus was arrested and the mob was screaming for blood, the cowering "Rock" was the disciple who denied Jesus three times and would not even acknowledge that he knew him.

After the crucifixion, when Jesus appeared to the disciples who were fishing by the Sea of Tiberias, Jesus asked the "Rock": "Simon, do you love me?" and when the Rock insisted that he did, Jesus replied, "Feed my sheep."

The Rock later went cheerfully about the business of feeding the Lord's sheep, and when he followed Jesus to a similar death, he went cheerfully to be crucified upside down.

Speaking to the Jews of Jerusalem at Pentecost, Peter said that David foresaw the resurrection of Jesus with these words: "I saw the Lord before me always, for with him at my right hand nothing can shake me. So *my heart was glad and my tongue cried out for joy*" (Acts 2:25–26).

A spirit of joy permeates the Acts of the Apostles, and Peter also imparted joy to those he encountered. When Peter was delivered from Herod's prison, he went to the house of Mary, the mother of John Mark. "He knocked at the outside door and a servant called Rhoda came to answer it. She recognized Peter's voice and was *so overcome with joy* that, instead of opening the door, she ran inside with the news that Peter was standing at the main entrance" (Acts 12:13–14).

Depressives and old grouches don't generally give other people such great joy.

In his letter to dispersed Christians in Galatia, Asia, and elsewhere, Peter spoke of *"a joy so glorious that it cannot be described."* "This is a cause of *great joy* for you, even though you may for a short time have to bear being plagued by all sorts of trials; so that when Jesus Christ is revealed, your faith will have been tested and proved like gold . . . You did not see him, yet you love him; and still without seeing him, you are already filled with *a joy so glorious that it cannot be described*, because you believe; and you are sure of the end to which your faith looks forward, that is, the salvation of your soul" (1 Pet. 1:6–9).

In the same letter, Peter said, "If you can have some share in the suffering of Christ, *be glad*, because you will enjoy *a much greater gladness* when his glory is revealed" (1 Pet. 4:13–14).

Other Joyful Apostles

The author of the epistles of John spoke of joy at the beginning of every one of his three letters.

"We are writing this to you to make our own *joy* complete" (1 John 1:4).

In the second letter, he declares at the start, "It has given me *great joy* to find that your children have been living the life of truth as we were commanded by the Father" (2 John 4), and he concludes, "I hope instead to visit you and talk to you personally so that our *joy* may be complete" (2 John 12).

The third letter, addressed to his friend Gaius, again opens by speaking of his joy: "It was a *great joy* to me when some brothers came and told of your faithfulness to the truth, and of your life in the truth. It is always *my greatest joy* to hear that my children are living according to the truth" (3 John 3–4).

The letter of James speaks repeatedly of happiness. It begins: "My brothers, you will always have your trials but, when they come, try to treat them as *a happy privilege*" (James 1:2–3). Later it declares, "*Happy* the man who stands firm when trials come" (James 1:12). "If any one of you is in trouble, he should pray; if anyone is feeling *happy*, he should sing a psalm" (James 4:13–14).

The letter of Jude concludes with these words: "Glory

be to him who can keep you from falling and bring you safe to his glorious presence, innocent and *happy*" (Jude 24–25).

Wherever the apostles went, they brought joy with them. Philip, preaching the good news in Samaria, worked many healing miracles. The mentally ill, paralytics, and cripples were cured through his prayers and loving care. "As a result, there was *great rejoicing* in that town" (Acts 12:13–14).

In Revelations, there are visions of catastrophe, but there are also visions of joy. "And I seemed to hear the voices of a huge crowd, like the sound of the ocean or the great roar of thunder, answering 'Alleluia! The reign of the Lord our God Almighty has begun; *let us be glad and joyful* and give praise to God, because this is the time for the marriage of the Lamb' " (Rev. 19:7–8).

Pietro Dacquino observes, "Joy also characterizes the encounters among the members of various [early] Christian communities. We are struck by the repeated exhortation to gladness and joy found especially in some of the apostolic writings. It is the joy already experienced by Christ himself, and is a gift of God from whom it directly derives."

The spirit of joy of the early Christians took practical expression in the many feast days and festive occasions they celebrated. The joyous feast days honoring various saints developed into tradition in the Roman Catholic and Orthodox churches. "The Christian feast is essentially a joyous remembrance of the Lord's death and resurrection," according to Benedictine Frederic Debuyst of Belgium. "Festive joy is a joy drawn from the Spirit, a Pentecostal joy."

In an article called "Joy and the Cross," Hans Urs von Balthasar, the Swiss theologian, writes, "Christianity is a 'joyful message.' . . . Its essential note must therefore incontestably be joy. . . . Christian joy retains such a particular burning, devouring element. Paul, in his words of comfort, can promise his suffering fellow Christians a pure, calm joy—just as Jesus promises pure, calm joy to his disciples in his words of farewell . . . "

Traditionally, the Christian liturgical year reaches its joyous peak at Easter, when Christians celebrate the resurrection. But even Lenten disciplines and fast days and the giving up of certain foods have been associated with joy. The Orthodox theologian Bishop Kallistos Ware observes, "Paradoxical though it may seem, the period of Lent is a time not of gloom but of joyfulness. It is true that fasting brings us to repentance and to grief for sin, but this penitent grief, in the vivid phrase of St. John Climacus, is a 'joy-creating sorrow.' "

For what should be the response of a man or woman who has been delivered from the jaws of hell? Thankfulness. Praise. Exultant joy. And, yes, even laughter.

Chapter 7

GOD'S GLAD MARTYRS

When I began writing it, I thought this would be the shortest chapter in the book. But, after studying the lives of Christian martyrs, I was surprised to discover how many of them endured persecution and torture with a cheerful heart, and how many faced even death with a radiant spirit of joy.

When we look at the lives of the saints and martyrs, we all too often see only their sufferings, their pain, their tears, their depressions, their struggles with the "dark night of the soul." But almost all of them had a light side, and many of them had a keen sense of humor. Some of the martyrs laughed in the face of their tormentors and executioners. Some of them smiled or jested shortly before they were beheaded, thrown to the lions, crucified, hanged, or burned to death.

This chapter can touch on only some of the many Christian martyrs who were persecuted and died for their beliefs. The saints in this chapter are Eastern Orthodox and/or Roman Catholic martyrs, but in my opinion, many of them—especially the martyrs of the early centuries—are also saints for Protestants to honor. For if it were not for their faith and sacrifices, Christianity would not have survived, and Protestants would never have received the Bible or other spiritual treasures. Many Protestants were later to be no less brave and joyful in the face of martyrdom. But our focus in this chapter is on the earlier Christian martyrs.

Unless otherwise indicated, the references are taken from Alban Butler's *Lives of the Saints*, revised and supplemented by Herbert Thurston and Donald Attwater.

Smiles in the Company of Lions

An early church martyr, Ignatius of Antioch (d. A.D. 107), a disciple of John the Evangelist, was bishop of Antioch when he was ordered arrested by the Roman emperor and brought to Rome. Ignatius was beloved as a healer who saw that "there is one Physician, of flesh and of spirit, son of Mary and son of God, Jesus Christ Our Lord," and who spoke of the Eucharist as "the flesh of Christ" and "the medicine of immortality." He was a humble and gentle man who was endlessly urging upon the divided early Christians unity of belief and spirit, but he emphasized the need of indulgence, patience, and forbearance toward the erring.

When the Roman soldiers arrived to arrest him, Ignatius "joyfully submitted his limbs to the fetters." Informed that he would be fed to the lions in Rome, Ignatius declared, "I have joy of the beasts that are prepared for me," so eager was he to follow in Christ's path and attain the crown of martyrdom.

Two lions in the Flavian amphitheater devoured him immediately, leaving only a few large bones.

Another disciple of John the Evangelist, St. Polycarp (d. A.D. 155), was bishop of Smyrna when he was ordered arrested by King Herod, who demanded that he deny the Christian faith or be burned at the stake. "Why do you delay?" replied Polycarp. "Bring against me what you please."

A witness observed that "whilst he said this, he appeared in a transport of joy and confidence, and his countenance shown with a certain heavenly grace." Polycarp was burned at the stake and pierced with a spear.

In Carthage in A.D. 203, five young catechumens were arrested as Christians and imprisoned. An account in Greek by one of them, a young woman named Perpetua, survives. St. Perpetua, who was carrying a small baby, wrote that after the judge "condemned us to the wild beasts, we returned joyfully to our prison."

In prison, one of the martyrs, St. Saturus, had a vision in which he and his companions were taken by angels to a beautiful garden, where they met many martyrs. "Then they were led to a place which seemed as though it were built of light, and sitting in it was One white-haired, but with the face of a youth. And on his right and on his left and behind him were many elders, and all sang with one voice: 'Holy, Holy, Holy.' We stood before the throne, and we kissed him and he passed his hand over our faces. We gave the kiss of peace. And the elders said to us, 'Go and play.' Then Saturus said to me: 'You have all you desired,' and I replied: 'Thanks be to God that as I was merry in the flesh, so am I still merrier here.' Saturus said, 'We began to recognize many brethren and martyrs there, and in joy I awoke.' " On the day they were thrown to the wild beasts, the five believers "set forth from the prison as though they were on their way to heaven. Perpetua was singing a psalm of triumph."

Another priest of Smyrna, St. Pionius and his friend, the Christian St. Sabina, suffered the same fate cheerfully about A.D. 250, smiling at their tormentors. "When Sabina heard threats that they would all be burnt alive, she only smiled. The pagans said, 'Dost thou smile? Then thou shalt be sent to the public stews.' She answered: 'God will be my protector there.' "

An eyewitness said of St. Pionius, "His face was radiant all the while the flames were rising about him and he gave up his spirit peacefully and painlessly to the Father. When the fire was put out, we who stood by saw that his body was like the well-cared-for body of a lusty athlete: the hair on his head and cheeks was not singed, and on his face there shone a wondrous radiance."

Another victim of the Valerian persecution, St. Laurence (d. A.D. 258), was a deacon in the Roman church who, when he heard he was to be arrested, "was full of joy . . . and gave everything to the poor."

He refused to deny the faith or sacrifice to idols. He was stripped, bound, and placed on a large gridiron above burning coals. After suffering a long time, he turned to the judge and said with a cheerful smile, "Let my body be turned; one side is broiled enough." After he was turned, he said, "It is cooked enough. You may eat," and then he died.

During the same persecution, Ss. Montanus, Luicius, and their companions (d. A.D. 259) "walked cheerfully to the place of execution and each one gave exhortations to the people." Before he was executed, Montanus told the crowd that "they might discern the true church by the multitude of its martyrs."

St. Fructuosus, bishop of Tarragon, Spain (d. A.D. 259), was roused from bed and arrested, along with two companions, under orders of the Roman emperor. Condemned to be burned alive, "the martyrs exulted to behold themselves on the verge of glorious eternity."

St. Agnes (d. A.D. 304) was courted by numerous Roman noblemen attracted by her beauty and riches, but she consecrated herself to Jesus. During the Diocletian persecution, she was condemned to be beheaded. St. Ambrose wrote, "Agnes, filled with joy on hearing this sentence, went to the place of execution more cheerfully than others go to their wedding."

One of the bravest of the early Christian martyrs was St. Vincent of Saragossa, a deacon and a contemporary of St. Agnes (d. A.D. 304). When he refused to deny the faith, Vincent "was first stretched on the rack by his hands and feet, and whilst he hung, his flesh was torn with iron hooks. Vincent, smiling, called the executioners weak and faint-hearted."

His persecutors then rubbed his wounds with salt, and put him on a gridiron of red-hot fire with bars full of spikes. Witnesses reported that "Vincent mounted cheerfully the iron bed."

Augustine wrote that Vincent suffered torments beyond what any man could have endured unless supported by a supernatural strength. He observed that "the more Vincent suffered, the greater seemed to be the inward joy and consolation of his soul."

St. Philip, bishop of Heraclea, also was martyred in A.D. 304. A crowd attacked him on the way to prison and threw him to the ground, but "he got up again with a smiling face," and he and his companions "went joyfully to the stake."

The Comedian Martyr and the Emperor

The Diocletian persecutions of the early fourth century were especially cruel. An unusual story is told of a confrontation between a comedian and the Emperor Diocletian, who had come to Rome.

In a theater, a comedy was given to entertain the pagan emperor. One of the comedians, a pagan named Genesius, lay down on the stage, pretended to be ill, and cried out, "I am resolved to die a Christian." Actors playing a Christian priest and exorcist were called. Genesius told them, "I desire to be born again and to be delivered from my sins."

The actors went through a mock Christian baptismal ceremony, and then actors playing soldiers seized Genesius and presented him to the emperor.

While speaking his lines, however, Genesius had been converted suddenly, and he told Diocletian very seriously, "Hear, O Emperor, I am truly a Christian," and he urged the audience to accept Jesus Christ as their Lord and obtain forgiveness of their sins.

The emperor supposed Genesius was still acting, but when the comedian continued to insist that he was a Christian, the emperor became enraged and ordered him beaten, tortured, and finally, beheaded.

One of the most famous of the early martyrs, St. Cecilia, became the patron saint of music and musicians. When she was arrested for her Christian activities, she was brought before a Roman judge who tried to induce her to sacrifice to pagan gods. "She laughed in his face," and playfully "tripped him up in his words." She, too, was beheaded.

St. Anastasius the Persian (d. A.D. 628) was a Persian soldier who became a Christian. He was arrested and tortured, and his persecutors told him he could go free if he denied Christ "just once." Anastasius refused, saying, "I go willingly and cheerfully to suffer for Christ," whereupon he was strangled and beheaded.

When in A.D. 859 the Moors were persecuting the Christians of Cordova, a Christian named Eulogius was brought before a judge who threatened to have him whipped to death. Eulogius is said to have replied with a smile, "If you could but conceive the reward which awaits those who persevere in the faith until the end, you would resign your dignities in exchange for it." He was beheaded.

There are, no doubt, many more merry martyrs following the conquest of the Moors, but it isn't until the sixteenth century that another preeminent historical figure good-naturedly went to his death.

St. Thomas More: The Martyr as Wit

St. Thomas More might well be the wittiest of all the Christian martyrs. Raymond E. F. Larsson, author of *Saints at Prayer*, observes that More was noted for "valuing highly wit and others' laughter."

More was a layman who considered becoming a Franciscan Friar Minor, but who instead married. He enjoyed a happy marriage and four children with his first wife.

His family met together daily for evening prayers, and at all meals the scriptures were read, followed by a lot of joking and jesting. He often invited his poorer neighbors to his table, but rarely the rich or the nobility.

After his beloved first wife died, he married a widow who helped care for his children. His only complaint against his second wife was that she did not appreciate his jokes.

He was a controversial writer, and some complained that his writing was "insufficiently solemn," but he "always preferred ridicule to denunciation."

More needed a sense of humor to be lord chancellor of England and counselor to King Henry VIII. When the king put away his queen to marry Anne Boleyn, More refused to sanction the marriage and was forced to resign as chancellor.

He and his family were reduced to poverty. He called his family together and lightheartedly explained their difficult position: "Then may we yet with bags and wallets go a-begging together, and hoping that for pity some good folk will give us charity, at every man's door to sing 'Salve regina,' and so still keep company and *be merry together."*

Henry VIII's insistence on marrying Anne Boleyn finally resulted in More's imprisonment in the Tower of London and the separation of England from the Roman Catholic Church.

In prison, More and his daughter watched three monks go to their execution. "Lo!" he said to her, "dost thou not see, Meg, that these blessed fathers be now as cheerfully going to their deaths as bridegrooms to their marriage?"

At his trial, denying that "a temporal lord could or ought to be head of spirituality," More told his judges, "I shall right heartily pray that though your lordships have now here on earth been judges of my condemnation, we may yet hereafter in heaven *merrily* all meet together to everlasting salvation."

He was good-humored, forgiving, and witty to the very end. He encouraged the headsman, covered his own eyes, and playfully adjusted his beard. At the scaffold, Larsson observes, "he found a jest to dull the edge of the headsman's axe." "I pray thee," More told the man who was about to behead him, "see me safe up, and for my coming down let me shift for myself." He died in 1535 at the age of fifty-seven.

There were later to be many more English martyrs, many of them victims of Cromwell's Puritans. Margaret

Clitherow of York, a laywoman "full of wit, very merry and loved by everyone" was imprisoned in 1586 for attending a mass. A contemporary wrote, "Her high spirits never forsook her, and when two days later she was joined by Mrs. Ann Tesh, the two friends joked and laughed together."

The judge ordered that she be pressed to death. She would be forced to lie on the ground while a door was placed over her and extremely heavy weights placed on the door. While she was en route to her death, "all marvelled to see her joyful, smiling countenance."

In 1642, the English Catholic priest Thomas Reynolds was sentenced to death for his priesthood, along with a monk, Alban Roe. Reynolds and Roe went to their hanging as if they were going to a party. On a cart en route to the scaffold, the monk turned to the priest and asked, "Well, how do you find yourself now?"

"In very good heart," replied Reynolds. "Blessed be God for it, and glad I am to have for my comrade in death a man of your undaunted courage."

At the scaffold, they gave each other absolution and forgave those who were about to hang them. Roe, who had been ministering to three felons who also were to die, turned to the people and remarked cheerfully, "Here's a jolly company!" His last word was a joking remark to one of the prison turnkeys.

Volumes of books could not do justice to the hundreds of thousands of Christian men and women, known and unknown—Catholic, Orthodox, and Protestant—who suffered martyrdom for their faith, either at the hands of unbelievers or of intolerant believers. Many were martyred in Nazi Germany and in Communist Russia, in Ireland, Poland, China, the Middle East, Central America. And they are still being martyred in many places around the world. It is difficult for us, living comfortably in America, to comprehend the depths of their sorrow or the heights of their joy.

The martyred Archbishop Oscar Romero of San Salvador, slain by an assassin's bullet five years ago while giving a homily at Mass, once wrote, "It is wrong to be sad. Christians cannot be pessimists. Christians must always nourish in their hearts the fullness of joy. Try it, brothers and sisters; i have tried it many times and in the darkest moments, when slander and persecution were at their worst: to unite myself intimately with Christ, my friend . . . It is the deepest joy the heart can have."

There is an old saying that the blood of the martyrs is the seed of the church. But we hardly ever hear of the joy of the martyrs. It was a contagious joy, and the early Christians, especially, had it in abundance, passing it on from generation to generation.

Chapter 8

THE HOLY LAUGHING SAINTS: CATHOLIC, ORTHODOX, AND PROTESTANT

Back in the sixteenth century, Francis de Sales, who did not know then that he was going to become the patron saint of Catholic journalists, expressed concern because contemporary biographers of the saints were giving an unreal picture of them by focusing only on their virtues. It was clear to de Sales that saints may have any number of faults and do any number of foolish things.

"There is no harm done to the saints if their faults are shown as well as their virtues," de Sales said. "But greater harm is done to everybody by those hagiographers who slur over the faults, be it for the purpose of honouring the saints . . . or through fear of diminishing our reverence for their holiness. These writers commit a wrong against the saints and against the whole of posterity."

Now, however, the pendulum has swung in the other direction. Whereas in the past, writers would draw unreal pictures of saints, showing only their virtues, now very often their faults are stressed to the exclusion of their virtues. Some psychiatrists and psychologists, with lofty disdain, have written books and articles for learned journals, suggesting that many of the saints were "schizophrenic," "depressive," "manic-depressive" "paranoid," etc.—in short, crazy.

There is some truth to claims that many of the saints suffered through periods in their lives when they appeared to be in the grasp of unrelenting depression, great anxiety, and illness of mind and body. For instance, Butler tells us that as a young monk, St. Ignatius of Loyola, founder of the Jesuits, "was soon visited with the most terrible trial of fears and scruples. His soul was overwhelmed with sadness. He apprehended some sin in every step he took, and seemed often on the very brink of despair."

What is significant, however, is that Ignatius patiently endured and triumphed over the trial of his depressive illness through prayer and keeping the faith. In time of trial, he continued to follow the way of his healing Lord, and his suffering eventually was transformed into joy. It was during his long depressive episode that Ignatius began to write material for his famous book, *Spiritual Exercises*. The Lord brought Ignatius out of his depression, restored his tranquillity of mind, "and his soul overflowed with spiritual joy."

Ignatius later would advise his seminarians: "Laugh and grow strong." He encouraged them to be merry of heart. A lover of billiards and chess, he also advised his students to take up sports and recreation as a balance to their studies.

The saints often were helped to vanquish their depressions and ailments by wise, patient, and good-humored spiritual directors (many of them laypeople), and confessors at monasteries, convents, and church retreat centers. Recovery was facilitated through a simple, moderate, and disciplined way of life that included worship, daily commu-

nion, prayer, periods of work, scriptural study, rest, recreation, and service—all in a setting close to nature's peace
and beauty. They also had the fellowship and support of
like-minded people. Their faith in Christ led to their complete healing or gave them the strength to bear their ailment cheerfully.

A few years ago, a friend who is an internationally esteemed psychiatrist and researcher astonished me by ex-
claiming, in a moment of exasperation over the "revolving
door policy" and bunglings of our high-priced secular psychiatric institutions, that the mentally and emotionally ill
were better off when they were under the care of monasteries, convents, and church retreat centers.

For years I wrote on psychiatric topics and was a director of a psychiatric research foundation, and it seemed to
me that many of the discoveries of our modern psychiatric
researchers and clinicians are simply confirmations of the
teachings of the Bible, the church fathers and mothers, and
the saints.

Not long ago, I attended a retreat at Holy Trinity Greek
Orthodox Church in Phoenix, Arizona, conducted by Rev.
George Vlahos, a psychologist and colleague of the distinguished psychotherapist Victor Frankl. "Everything in the
psychotherapeutic world," observed Vlahos, "can be
traced to the Bible. And there was no greater psychiatrist
than Jesus Christ."

I suspect that a study of the lives of the saints would
provide ample evidence that the church's monasteries, convents, and retreat centers may well have done a better job
of rehabilitating the depressed, brokenhearted, and emotionally disturbed than do our modern secular mental and
psychiatric institutions. And they certainly were a lot less
costly. I suspect that our mental health professionals could

learn a great deal about the compassionate care of the depressed and emotionally ill by studying the writings of the great monastic spiritual directors and confessors.

The monasteries and convents were spiritual healing centers that took in a lot of depressed neurotics and transformed them into joyful saints who contributed greatly to the well-being of the societies in which they lived. Many of the saints themselves became healers who were especially renowned for their ability to calm and heal the mentally and emotionally ill.

It is a great irony, however, that while many of the saints were able to heal others with a prayer, a touch, or a word, they were not always able to heal themselves of their own ailments, and some of them sought the help of doctors and clergy.

Many saints spoke both wisely and foolishly. But is there a man or woman anywhere who does not speak both wisdom and foolishness?

The saints saw Christ in every person they met. Their view was quite different from those Christians who see demons in everyone but themselves, and who love to denounce as "satanic" anyone who does not agree with them one hundred percent. The saints humbly conceded that they, too, were little devils on occasion and not worthy of the Lord's mercy.

In both the secular and religious press today, saints are often pictured as solemn, sullen, sorrowful, melancholy, anguished, judgmental, stern, harsh, sickly, or just plain kooky.

More than a score of years ago, in an article called "The Wit of Saints" in *Vogue* magazine, Phyllis McGinley complained that "pious writers" have drawn saints "all soul and no body. They pose them in plaster attitudes, hands forever uplifted, eyes cast down. They forget that what a reader wants is not a picture, but a motion picture. The stir of life is missing, and so is the sound of a natural voice: the sight of failure, the murmur of discontent, the ripple of laughter. Most of all I miss the laughter.

"Yet I am certain it is there. The dedicated [saint] watcher, if he listens long enough, can hear it all about him, a delicate tintinnabulation of joyousness as old as sainthood. In forests of virtue, the very branches quiver with gentle hilarity. And staring, one sees the saints shake off their carven poses and begin to move merrily like men and women . . . During the process of canonization, the Catholic Church demands proof of joy in the candidate. It is a pity that hagiographers have not kept this point more in mind . . . Wit is not the prerogative of the unjust: there is laughter in holy places."

How about all the saints who were known, to those who loved and followed them, for their cheerful disposition, wit, and hearty good humor? The truth is that, though many of them engaged in spiritual warfare with depression, most of the saints regarded cheerfulness as a virtue and valued a sense of humor.

De Sales himself was a charming and eloquent wit who got a law degree before becoming a priest. He enjoyed giving religious instruction to children, and, Knowles reports, his "classes were often jolly affairs, punctuated by laughter as the bishop illustrated a serious point with a funny story."

It was de Sales who said: "A saint who is sad is a sad saint."

I am far from being an authority on saints. But I do know that it is the habit of churches to venerate their saints and prophets of the past and to spurn their contemporary ones as pests or mad people. I also know that saints differ greatly in their personalities and style.

For instance, the story is told that God allowed the founders of three Catholic religious orders—the Franciscans, the Benedictines, and the Jesuits—to be present at the birth of Christ.

St. Francis and St. Benedict were overwhelmed by the majesty of the event and fell to their knees and prayed quietly.

But St. Ignatius Loyola, founder of the Jesuits, looked at the infant in the manger and took Joseph aside.

"Have you given any thought to the boy's education?" he asked.

Catholic and Orthodox Saints

Chances are you never heard of Philip Neri. He was a sixteenth-century Catholic clown-priest who was the delight of the people of Rome. Butler calls him "the most unconventional of saints."

Neri was a lifelong vegetarian and a constant clown who lived to a ripe old age. Like many clowns, he had both the gift of tears and the gift of laughter. As a young seminarian, he used to weep whenever he saw the large crucifix in the college chapel.

He became a priest and was renowned as a confessor in Rome, serving the lowly, the cardinals, and the popes. He became one of the most popular men in Rome. Crowds lined up to confess to him, even though he imposed some wild and crazy penances.

Leo Knowles observes, "Philip was not mad, as those who joined his merry band quickly discovered. Catherine of Siena and Teresa of Avila loved gaiety and used it to help others to get to heaven. Philip's antics served the same purpose, but he went a stage further. He became a buffoon.

"Solemnity he treated as if it were a vice. In Philip's

eyes, any form of holiness which did not leave room for laughter was gravely suspect."

Neri was a confessor to Caesar Baronius, a very sullen and melancholy cardinal, and once, as a penance, Neri required the cardinal to sing the "Miserere" at a wedding. It cured the cardinal of his gloomy habit. As another penance, Neri once required a proud young man to go out into the heat of summer wearing a heavy fur coat to cure him of his pride.

It is said that the two books he most valued were the New Testament and a book of jokes. He once told a group of young people who came to listen to him: "I will have no sadness in my house."

Neri, wearing white shoes, often was seen walking around Rome, laughing and singing, followed by his jovial friends and his fat white dog. Rome's little street urchins loved him, as he loved them, and they often waited to catch a glimpse of him and to share a laugh with him.

"Everywhere Philip went, people laughed," according to Knowles. "There was no end to the mad things he did." Once, Neri shaved half his beard off and toured the streets of Rome as a half-bearded priest.

He frequently visited the sick in hospitals, "always with the same friendly smile, and the same friendly greeting."

Neri once cured Pope Clement of gout simply by shaking hands with him, one of the many cures that were attributed to him. Shortly before he died in 1595, he "appeared to be in a radiantly happy mood, bordering on exultation."

But let's return to the early Christians, and move forward from there to modern times.

Defending the Faith with Wit

The early church leaders were not reluctant to defend

the faith with wit. Needling the initiation practices of the gnostics, Irenaeus, bishop of Lyons (d. A.D. 203), declared, "As soon as a man has been won over to their way of salvation, he becomes so puffed up with conceit and self-importance that he imagines himself to be no longer in heaven or on earth, and with the majestic air of a cock, he goes strutting about as if he had already embraced his angel."

Gregory, a bishop in Palestine (268), "had a formidable power over evil spirits," according to Basil. He "organized secular amusements in connection with the commemorations of the martyrs," believing that "the martyrs were honoured by happy recreation in addition to formal religious observances."

The great monastic Jerome (d. A.D. 420) also had a ready smile and a ready wit. He once described a critic of the Christians as "big and fat, a fellow bloated with Scots porridge." Criticizing some of the clergy of Rome and Antioch, Jerome observed, "All their anxiety is about their clothes . . . You would take them for bridegrooms rather than for clerics; all they think about is to know the names and houses and doings of rich ladies."

From his monastic retreat, he wrote a friend, "I amuse myself by laughing at the grubs, owls, and crocodiles."

St. Martin's troublesome deacon, Brice, called him crazy, but Martin, bishop of Tours (d. A.D. 444), refused to dismiss him, saying, "If Christ could tolerate Judas, surely I can tolerate Brice." Brice later succeeded Martin and became an exemplary bishop.

Chrysostom: Joyful Mouth of Gold

St. John Chrysostom, patriarch of Constantinople (d. A.D. 407), was a liturgical genius and an eloquent orator who was known as "the mouth of gold" by the Antiochians and Greeks whom he served. Though his own health was fragile, Chrysostom was keenly aware of the healing power of humor and of a cheerful attitude. In one of his homilies, called "Rejoice in the Lord Always," Chrysostom observed that "he who fears the Lord enjoys a continued tranquillity and laughs to scorn all things which seem to be sorrowful. It is not the nature of things, but our disposition which is want to make us sad or joyful."

In his famous Easter midnight homily, inviting everybody to the feast of the Eucharist, Chrysostom declared, "If a man is a wise servant, let him with rejoicing enter into the *joy* of his Lord . . . and he that hath arrived only at the eleventh hour, let him not be afraid by reason of his delay; for the Lord is gracious and receiveth the last even as the first. He giveth rest to him that cometh at the eleventh hour as well as to him that hath toiled from the first. Let all then enter into the *joy* of our Lord. Let no one mourn that he hath fallen again and again, for forgiveness hath risen from the grave."

Chrysostom further exclaimed, "Hell was angered when it encountered Thee [Christ] in the lower regions; Hell was angered, for it was abolished; Hell was angered for it was mocked."

By the dictionary, "mock" means to ridicule with laughter, and the image Chrysostom presented here is of Jesus descending into hell and taunting it with his laughter as he breaks its gates and delivers the imprisoned spirits. It is the image of Christ confronting the Devil and laughing at him.

At the end of Chrysostom's Divine Liturgy, the priest prays, "O Christ our God, who are thyself the fulfillment of the law and the prophets, who didst fulfill all the dispensation of the Father: *fill our hearts with joy and gladness, always:* now and ever and unto ages of ages. Amen."

Chrysostom was unfailingly gentle with sinners and the poor and sick. "If you have fallen a second time, or even a thousand times, into sin, come to me and you shall be healed," he wrote.

There are many beautiful liturgies in the Christian world, but none, I think, more beautiful than Chrysostom's Divine Liturgy. After seventeen centuries, the liturgy still has great healing power when sung and chanted in English so that people can understand it.

His liturgy is by turns solemn and joyous. Everything in the liturgy—the words, poetry, hymns, images—is positive, edifying, comforting, encouraging, focused on a good, loving, compassionate, merciful, endlessly forgiving God who heals those who seek him. Interestingly, in the entire liturgy, there is not a single mention of the Devil.

Chrysostom delivered such brilliant and witty homilies that people often broke out into enthusiastic applause in the middle of the worship service. This grieved Chrysostom, a humble man, and thereafter he instructed all the clergy to give their sermons at the very end of the service, so that the focus of the service would always be fixed on the Lord, not on the clergy.

Apollo (d. A.D. 394) was the abbot of a monastery. He daily exhorted his monks to three things: (1) humility; (2) daily holy communion; and (3) a cheerful attitude of mind. "He insisted often on the evils of melancholy and sadness, saying that cheerfulness of heart is necessary amidst our tears of penance as being the fruit of charity, and requisite to maintain the spirit of fervour. He himself was known to strangers by the joy of his countenance."

Apollo also was a healer, and many astonishing miracles are recorded of him, especially the healing of the mentally ill. Butler observes that on one occasion, "when the devil quitted a possessed person at his command, the evil spirit cried out that he was not able to withstand his humility." Possibly the same was true of his good humor. He lived to well over ninety.

Augustine (d. A.D. 430) spoke to God of his life ebbing and flowing between tears and laughter: "Now I am merry, and anon I am sad; now I am strong, and anon I am weak; now I am alive, and by and by I am dead. I seem happy for a while, and I always am wretched: one while I laugh, and another while I weep . . . In Thee doth my soul rejoice."

Augustine wrote a dialogue called *Of the Happy Life*, and both as a priest and as a bishop, he is reputed to have been able, through prayer, to drive evil spirits from the possessed. Like Ambrose, he faced his last illness with great cheerfulness. While he lay sick in bed, he is said to have healed a sick man by the laying on of hands.

Faces Which Smiled on All Mankind

The high-spirited St. Brigid (d. A.D. 525) is regarded by the Irish "as the patroness of all good women to whom Erin has given birth." A spirit of joy was Brigid's companion, and many of the ill were healed in her presence or through her prayers. *The Book of Lismore* declares, "Everything that Brigid asked of the Lord was granted her at once. For this was her desire: to satisfy the poor, to expel every hardship, to spare every miserable man."

Another revered Irish saint, St. Ita (d. A.D. 570) ran a school for boys. One day a youngster asked her "the three things which God most abhors."

She replied: "A *face which scowls upon all mankind*, obstinacy in wrong-doing, an overweening confidence in the power of money. These are three things which are hateful in God's sight."

Orthodox Bearers of Joy

In some parts of Greece, we've been told, it is a very old local custom in the Greek Orthodox Church to observe the Monday after Easter (Pascha) as a day of laughter—to celebrate the practical joke that God played on Satan by raising Christ from the dead. From the fourth century onwards, the holy fool has been a recurring figure in Greek and Russian Christianity.

The fools were regarded as holy men and women and as prophets, and the high and low sought their counsel and their blessings. Some of them seemed to be mad, and ironically, the prayers of holy fools often were sought for the mentally ill and credited with healing them.

St. Symeon of Emesa, a sixth-century monk, is the best-known holy fool in the Greek tradition. (Most of the Russian fools, however, were not monks but rather homeless wanderers.) The well-educated son of wealthy Greek parents, Symeon became a monk and spent thirty years in continual prayer in the desert near the Jordan. One day, Symeon, now about fifty, announced to a fellow monk: "What profit is it to us, brother, to spend our days here in the desert? But, if you will hearken to me, arise, let us go and save others as well. By the power of Christ, I am going to mock the world."

His brother monk declined the invitation, protesting: "I have not yet reached so high a level as this, to be able to mock the world."

Symeon went to Emesa in western Syria and began to play the part of a mad fool. One Sunday, he took some walnuts into church, and at the start of the service, he began to crack the nuts. He then went to the pulpit and tossed walnuts at the parishioners.

Symeon hopped and jumped around in the streets. Once, he took off all his clothes, wrapped them around his head, and ran into the women's section of the public baths. When a merchant hired him to peddle his food and drinks, Symeon gave away everything to the poor.

Symeon showed a special love for "demoniacs." Wrote Bishop Leontius of Neapolis, his biographer: "He shared in the suffering of those possessed by demons more than in the sufferings of any others. Often he went to them and behaved as if he were himself one of them; and passing his time with them, he healed many of them through his prayers."

Bishop Kallistos Ware, one of the foremost contemporary theologians and historians of the Orthodox Church, observes: "Symeon does not proffer aid from a safe distance. The fool's prayers confer healing because he has made his own all the anguish of those for whom he intercedes. Through this act of identification, he brings hope and healing. Like Christ, the fool goes out in search of the lost sheep and brings it back on his shoulders. He goes down into the pit to draw others out of it. Folly, for Symeon, was a way of showing love for others. Folly opened for him doors that otherwise would have remained closed. Had he simply gone into the taverns and brothels and delivered homilies, who would have listened? It was through his gentle companionship, through his playfulness and joy, that he moved the hearts of drunkards and prostitutes. Like Christ, the fool does not curse or condemn, and therein lies his power of attraction."*

According to Ware, "Genuine instances of folly for Christ's sake are exceedingly rare, and the spiritual tradi-

---

*Bishop Ware published a splendid article, "The Fool in Christ as Prophet and Apostle," *Sobornost* 6:2 (1984).

tion is unanimous in regarding this as an unusually perilous vocation. According to a recent emigre, holy fools are still to be found in Russia. They keep hidden and others hide them; if discovered, they are interred in psychiatric asylums. Modern tyrannies have reason to be afraid of the fool's freedom."

Bishop Ware believes that the church should "allow a place for the unconventional life-giving vocation" of the holy fool. . . . "May we always find room for the holy fool within our church communities; for the community that excludes the fool may find that it has also shut the door in the face of the Divine Fool, Christ himself."

St. John Climacus of Mount Sinai (d. A.D. 649) was a man of laughter who lived the century after Symeon, but continued the tradition of Orthodox joy. He wrote, "God does not insist or desire that we should mourn in agony of heart; rather it is his wish that out of love for him, we should rejoice with laughter in our soul."

John was an abbot upon whom "God bestowed an extraordinary grace of healing the spiritual disorder of souls." He once healed a monk of depression when they prostrated themselves and prayed together.

St. John of Damascus (d. A.D. 754), who composed many Orthodox hymns, offered this prayer for a Church festival: "Come, ye assembly of God-loving people . . . Let us raise the *shout of joy* with our lips, as with tuned cymbals! Come: let us exult in spirit! . . . To whom belong joy and gladness, if not to them that fear the Lord, that worship the Trinity? . . . It is for us that Christ has ordained the festivals, for '*there is no joy to the wicked.*' Let us lay aside the cloud of every grief that darkens our mind, and suffer it not to be raised on high. Let us make light of all earthly things, for our citizenship is not on the earth."

Not all of his fellow monks appreciated his joyful singing. A cranky old monk, with whom he shared a cell, once turned on him furiously and pushed him out of the cell. "Is this the way you forget your vows?" the old monk shouted. "Instead of mourning and weeping, you sit in joy and delight yourself by singing!"

St. Deicolus (d. A.D. 625) was an abbot in a French monastery. "Amidst his austerities, the joy and peace of his soul appeared in his countenance." A friend once asked him: "Deicolus, why are you smiling?"

"Because no one can take God from me," he answered.

An extraordinary story is told about a layman named St. Drithelm (d. A.D. 700), who died one evening and the next morning suddenly sat up. His wife and friends fled in terror, but he calmly told them not to be afraid, that he had been returned to life.

He said that when he died, a guide came and he was taken to a fiery pit, where he saw the souls of many people, including a priest, crying out in great torment. He then was permitted a glimpse of heaven: a flowery, fragrant place, full of light and singing and "beautiful young people so shining and merry." (Drithelm's description of heaven as being a "merry" place tallies with both earlier and later visions of it by other saints.)

His guide told him he would be given another opportunity to live a more virtuous life on earth, and he announced to his wife that he was going to become a monk. His wife's reaction is not recorded.

St. Bruno (d. A.D. 1101), the founder of the Carthusian Order, was known for his cheerful disposition. Butler cites a letter written by Bruno which shows that "gaiety of soul . . . is particularly necessary in all who are called to a life of solitude, in which nothing is more pernicious than sadness and to which nothing is more contrary than a tendency to morbid introspection." Psychoanalysis was not their pastime.

St. Bernard of Clairvaux (d. A.D. 1153), a great monastic reformer and founder of the Cistercians, was one of the most popular and compelling figures of the Middle Ages. Mothers hid their sons when they saw him coming. Wives hid their husbands, and girls their boyfriends. They were afraid that Bernard would make monks of them.

Bernard was very handsome, and he often was pestered by women. Once a young woman climbed naked into his bed. Bernard woke up, saw the girl, moved over to make room for her, turned on his side and went back to sleep. Now that is not only monkish discipline; it's a display of a fantastic sense of humor.

While opening a new abbey at Foigny, the Cistercian brothers were attacked by a horde of flies. They were unable to swat them away. Finally, Bernard solemnly told the flies, "I hereby excommunicate you." The next day, the story goes, every single fly was found dead on the floor.

Bernard once wrote to reassure the worried parents of a young man who had joined the Cistercian monastery. "Do not be sad about Geoffrey," Bernard wrote, "or weep for him. He is going swiftly to joy, not to sorrow."

Bernard once likened himself to a jester: "For what do we seem to worldlings to be doing but playing about, when we flee what they desire in this world and seek what they flee? We are like those jesters and tumblers, who, with heads down and feet up, reverse human habits by standing or walking on their hands, and so draw all eyes on them . . . Let us play this game that we may be made game of, confounded, humiliated, until he shall come who casts down the mighty and exalts the humble, who will gladden us, glorify us, and exalt us forever." Jean Leclercq observed, "It is part of St. Bernard's greatness that he could make fun of himself as God's jester."

Bernard was no stranger to depression, however. When he was a young man, his mother died and he became "morbidly despondent," but was "rallied out of his brooding and inertia" by his merry-hearted sister. Much of his life he suffered from stomach troubles, but it is said that he could cure sick persons instantly by making the sign of the cross on them. Erasmus described him as "cheerful and pleasant."

Before his conversion to Christianity, St. Vladimir of Kiev (d. A.D. 1015), the patron saint of Russia, was a wild and bloodthirsty tyrant who had five wives and many female slaves. The Chronicle of Nestor observed that the grand-prince's "desire for women was too much for him." Converted at the age of thirty-two, he put away all his wives and mistresses, married the Christian daughter of the Byzantine emperor, reformed his life, and supported the Greek Orthodox missionaries who eventually converted all of Russia.

The Chronicle of Nestor, noting that the wild Vladimir received God's grace and forgiveness, observed that "the Devil was overcome by fools and madmen, while many righteous and godly men strayed from their path of rightness and perished." Vladimir's merry disposition earned him the title "The Sunny Prince."

The Perfect Joy of St. Francis

Like Jesus, St. Francis of Assisi (d. A.D. 1226) wept from time to time, but joy and wit were Francis's trademarks, and he considered himself a "fool for Christ." "Where there is sadness," Francis often prayed, "let me sow your joy."

In his book *St. Francis*, Nikos Kazantzakis has the little saint asking, "Lord, where do I get the strength to sing and dance on this dunghill?"

"When Francis was among others," Kazantzakis writes, "he would laugh and frolic—would spring suddenly into the air and begin to dance, or would seize two sticks and play the viol while singing sacred songs he himself had composed. Doubtless he did so to encourage his companions . . . When he was alone, however, his tears began to flow."

Men and women by the thousands were attracted to Francis because of his joy and good spirits. G. K. Chesterton observed that in the thirteenth century, "men acted quite differently according to whether they had met him or not."

James J. Thompson, Jr., reviewing Chesterton's book on St. Francis in the *New Oxford Review*, observed, "Although he challenged men to dare the most stringent poverty, his asceticism radiated joy, even playfulness; St. Francis wanted his followers to laugh, not to waste their breath on sullen denunciations of materialism. He loved men, not humanity."

Francis died in 1226, welcoming his sweet "Sister Death" with, as an observer at the death scene reported, "the look of a smiling saint." Of course, Francis would be happy because he would soon be with God. "But," observed Thompson, "I think something else accounts for that smile as well: the little fool of Assisi, once derided and mocked by his townsmen, had turned the world upside down, and try as they might, the proud, the powerful, the arrogantly rich would never be able to restore it completely to their liking."

There is a story about Francis traveling with Brother Leo. The two were returning to their friary, and Leo asked Francis, "What is perfect joy?" Francis replied, "And if we continue to knock [at the door] and the brother porter comes out and drives us away with curses and hard blows—and if we bear it patiently, and take the insults with joy and love in our hearts, Oh, Brother Leo, write down that that is perfect joy!"

After the death of Francis, St. Clare (d. A.D. 1253) suffered from disabling illnesses for twenty-eight years and was often bedridden. But she still managed to found and direct the Poor Clares. She bore her ailments patiently and cheerfully, coming "from prayer with her face so shining that it dazzled the eyes of those that beheld her."

On her deathbed, Clare comforted a weeping brother who was concerned about the pain she was experiencing. "Dear brother," she said, "ever since by means of his servant Francis I have known the grace of our Lord Jesus Christ, I have never in my whole life found any pain or sickness that could afflict me."

A Third Order follower of Francis, St. Elizabeth of Hungary (d. A.D. 1231), was a very happily married woman who devoted much of her time to establishing hospitals. She had a playful sense of humor, and she once brought a leper home and laid him on the bed she shared with her husband. When her husband came home, he was furious, but all at once "he saw the figure of Christ crucified stretched upon the bed."

When her husband was killed in the Crusades, Elizabeth entered a convent and bore her grief with "that good self-confidence so often seen when a sense of humor serves submission to God."

Another early Third Order Franciscan, St. Angela (d. A.D. 1309) tried to follow Francis in a life of "joyful love." Widowed, she was "filled with anger, bitterness, and ill-nature" and fell into deep depression that lasted more than two years. "At last," Butler writes, "her poor tortured soul . . . was filled with . . . that joy which was the keynote of the early Franciscan life." When she recovered from her depression, she wrote that she was full of love—"even for devils," adding, "All is joy."

Francis's friend St. Dominic (d. A.D. 1221), founder of the Order of Preachers, spent a great deal of time in church as a young man, "weeping for the sins of others." As he grew in the faith, a contemporary observed that "it was easy to see from his friendly and joyous countenance that he was at peace inwardly."

Dominic's successor as head of the Dominicans was Jordan of Saxony (d. A.D. 1237). There is a story that Jordan once brought a group of young novices and postulants together in a friary for evening prayers. While Jordan was reading the office, one of the young men, under nervous strain, began to giggle. It was contagious and all the others began to giggle, too. One of the brothers tried, in vain, to stop them.

Jordan ignored them, finished the prayers, and gave them the blessing. Then he turned to the young men and said, "Laugh on! You may well laugh, for you have escaped the Devil who formerly held you in bondage. Laugh away, dear sons!"

Catherine of Siena Sees a Smiling Christ

St. Catherine of Siena (d. A.D. 1380) was described as being "very merry" as a girl. One day, she was walking home with her brother when she suddenly stopped spellbound, her eyes fixed on the sky. She would not respond to her brother's calls until finally he took her hand.

She burst into tears because the vision she had seen had

vanished. She said she had seen Jesus with Peter, Paul, and John, and Jesus had smiled at her and raised his hand to bless her. After that, she committed herself to serving the Lord.

Yet even in her own order, she was denounced by some as a fanatic or as a hypocrite. For a long time before her death, her health was fragile and she was never free of pain, "yet her emaciated face habitually bore a happy and even smiling expression, and her personal charm was as winning as ever."

"From Sullen Saints, Save Us, O Lord"

The sixteenth century produced a host of high-spirited and witty saints. St. Francis Xavier (d. A.D. 1522), one of the greatest of all missionaries, was renowned both for his courage and his "ready wit."

St. Teresa of Avila (d. A.D. 1582), founder of the Carmelites, was noted for an ironic sense of humor and a deft way of turning a phrase. She once suffered "extreme desolation of soul" (another term for depression) that was to last for three years, but she never lost her faith or her sense of humor. When a male admirer praised the beauty of her bare feet, she laughed and told him to take a good look at them because he would never see them again.

Butler speaks of "the liveliness of her wit and imagination." One day, Teresa was about to go on a trip, and she prayed to God for a safe journey. The trip was almost a disaster. There were delays, accidents, illness. When she returned, she went back to talk to God again, this time to complain.

Her complaint went something like this: "Lord, I prayed

to you for a safe and pleasant trip, and what do I get? I get nothing but problems."

God replied, "But Teresa, that's how I treat all my friends."

Teresa answered: "Yes, I know, and that's why you've got so few of them."

Teresa wrote many inspirational letters that sparkled with humor. When she counseled her nuns, she did so with wit. A young nun, very depressed, once came to her announcing, with some pride, that she was a great sinner.

Replied Teresa, "Sister, remember, none of us is perfect. Just make sure those sins of yours don't turn into bad habits."

Once a difficult abbess was getting on Teresa's nerves. Teresa prayed, "Lord, if I had my way that woman wouldn't be superior here." She wrote that the Lord answered her, "Teresa, if I had my way, she wouldn't be either."

It was Teresa who gave us these words: "From somber, serious, sullen saints, save us, O Lord. Lord, hear our prayer."

Smiling Saints of Recent Centuries

Sebastian Valfré (d. 1710) was a French priest renowned for his tenderness to the sick. He went through a long and hellish period of depression and inner turmoil, but when he recovered, he was known for being "always cheerful, so that men judged him to be light-hearted and free from care."

St. John Joseph of the Cross (d. 1734), a Franciscan novice-master, was a cheerful soul who insisted that novices and friars should have a daily schedule of recreation. He recognized that play was important as a balance to worship and work.

St. Emily de Rodat, founder of a convent in Villefranche (d. 1852), had a gift for amusing remarks. "There are some people who are not good for a convent," she once said, "but a convent is good for them; they would be lost in the world, and they don't do much good in a convent—but at least they keep out of mischief."

St. John Vianney (d. 1859) was a curé, a parish priest in France. (In calling a priest a "curé," the French historically have recognized the healing power of the clergy, for a curé is entrusted with the cure of souls.) Many healing miracles are associated with Vianney. It was said of Vianney that "when most interiorly moved, he simply smiled—or wept."

Like many reformers, St. Don John Bosco (d. 1888) was considered crazy by his opponents. His foes managed to persuade somebody high up in the church hierarchy that Bosco was a lunatic for taking in so many delinquent boys and orphans into his home and trying to run it without any financial backing.

Two priests drove up in a carriage one day and invited Bosco to take a drive into the country with them. But Bosco had been forewarned that the priests intended to take him to the lunatic asylum for examination.

He went to get his hat and coat but then stepped back and politely invited the two priests to get in the carriage before him. After the priests had seated themselves, he slammed the door behind them and shouted to the driver, "To the asylum!" The driver drove away.

One of the most extraordinary of the modern saints, St. Therese of Lisieux (d. 1897) was a fragile Carmelite who fought a running battle with illnesses much of her brief life.

Her right lung completely eaten away by tuberculosis, Therese died in a cloister in Lisieux, France, at the age of twenty-four. Notwithstanding the constant pain in which she lived, she always exhorted her sisters to be cheerful. "When we are with the sick, we must be cheerful," she would tell them. "After all, we mustn't lament like those who have no hope."

Her autobiography, *Story of a Soul*, later was translated into thirty-two languages, and touched the hearts of thousands. Therese, who called herself "God's Little Flower," appeared to soldiers dying on the battlefields of World War I, and was credited with letting roses come to thousands, including to Dorothy Day in midwinter in a New York slum.

James E. Milford, in the *Canadian Messenger of the Sacred Heart*, wrote: "Therese saw holiness in being cheerful when you did not wish to be, in keeping your pains and irritations to yourself. . . . She is a pillar of bright fire, a message of unselfish joy to a world trapped in selfish living."

The Laughing Confessor

The Abbé Henri de Tourville was a nineteenth-century French priest who spent himself with such absolute devotion and intensity as a confessor that his health broke down. He spent the remaining twenty years of his life an invalid whose greatest spiritual struggles were with depression. From his sickbed, he continued to write beautifully, however, and he became a spiritual adviser to many depressed and ill clergymen and laymen who sought his counsel.

De Tourville gave them precisely the opposite advice that many of our modern secular psychoanalysts and psychotherapists are giving their patients. He advised: Develop a sense of humor; don't take yourself too seriously; laugh at yourself; don't dwell on your past; don't look back; don't waste time and energy analyzing yourself.

In his *Letters of Direction*, de Tourville observed that the soul receives many wounds during its lifetime on earth. But he advised people not to dwell on their wounds, lest they become prisoners of the past.

"I cannot understand," de Tourville wrote one parishioner, "how in the presence of our Lord, anyone could go on thinking about himself, even if he were the last of men. The time has come when you must no longer think of yourself, but only of the compassion and love which Jesus has for you. Rejoice in this thought. From every point of view, we gain infinitely more by looking at our Lord than by looking at ourselves. We shake off our faults more quickly and effectively when we adore our Lord than when we examine and criticize ourselves.

"The soul gains very little from looking at itself. Such an occupation gives rise only to discouragement, preoccupation, distress, uncertainty, and illusion. Looking at our Lord, on the contrary, does us good, and we are gradually transfigured by His personality and by the spirit of imitation. When bit by bit you have given up scrutinizing your soul . . . then you will have made a great step forward and truly found God. We should be lighthearted, like those who think they have too much."

Comforting an anxious, depressed priest, de Tourville advised him to look upon himself as a soldier who has fallen wounded in combat. "Whatever makes life seem sad and melancholy to us is an error on our part, and we must realize it," de Tourville wrote the priest. "Our Lord is with us in all our troubles and always gives us sufficient help to carry us through. Smile and even laugh at yourself when you feel all this inner hubbub going on in you. It is the childish language of nature: plaintive, fearful, unreasonable. We always have it with us. It is a splendid habit to laugh inwardly at yourself. It is the best way of regaining your good humor and of finding God without further anxiety.''

Giuseppe Sarto (d. A.D. 1914) had a terrible temper as a young boy, but by the time he became Pope Pius X it had been transformed into what Leo Knowles calls "a puckish sense of humor."

He had the gift of healing, and many miraculous cures were attributed to his blessings, even over long distances. "They say I am working miracles, as though I had nothing else to do," he once joked.

He didn't like the custom of kissing the pope's foot and put an end to it. He told a cardinal who tried to kiss his foot, "Don't do that, my dear friend. I'm so afraid I might kick you in the nose!"

Modern Catholic and Orthodox Wits

The runners bearing the torch of Christian humor and joy often have stumbled and fallen through the centuries, but others have picked it up and taken their places.

Dr. John Eudes Bamberger, who knew Thomas Merton, says of Merton, "He was very human and available. He was a very freewheeling, outgoing person with an obvious ease with relationships, a very enthusiastic type of person. He really was very responsive to human suffering," and "he had a terrific sense of humor."

The beloved Pope John XXIII, whose large heart embraced all Christians, made this entry in his journal when he was still a seminarian. "The pure, refined joy which must always fill my heart finds its most sincere expression in the humblest actions. I must take care then: it is not enough to bear vexations with patience of a sort . . . I must always feel within myself an indescribable gentleness and sweetness that will bring a smile to my lips, and an even brighter smile when I am trying hard not to lose my temper and feeling rather grim. In short, I must show a cheerful, smiling patience, not too solemn or there is no merit in it."

According to Monsignor Arthur Tonne, Pope John XXIII had "a warm, down-to-earth sense of humor." One time a new building had to be constructed on Vatican grounds. The architect submitted the plans to His Holiness, who shortly afterward returned them with these three Latin words written in the margin: "Non sumus angeli," which mean "We are not angels."

The architect and his staff couldn't figure out what the pope meant, until finally, someone noticed that the plans did not include bathrooms.

The eminent priest-biologist Teilhard de Chardin observed that "joy is the infallible sign of the presence of God in anybody." He said that one must come to the Kingdom of God with the openness of a young child—"optimistic, active, smiling, perceptive."

That remarkable woman, Catherine de Hueck Doherty, a Russian immigrant who fled Communist Russia and founded Madonna House Apostolate in Combermere, Ontario, wrote in her book, *Poustinia*:

"If you ever see a sad hermit or poustinik*, then he is no hermit at all. The most joyful persons in Russia are the ones

---

*A *Poustinik* refers to someone dwelling in a secluded spot or a hermitage for the purpose of praying for one's sins and the sins of the world. The word *poustina*, another derivative of the same root, literally means "desert" in Russian.

who have the eyes of a child at seventy and who are filled with the joy of the Lord: the poustinikki, for they who have entered the silence of God are filled with God's joy. The life of a poustinik should be truly visible. He will have the eyes of a child even if his face is that of an old woman or man. You cannot fool people as to such things as the presence of love and joy in a human being."

Although some Christians in affluent America find little or nothing to smile about, the Holy Spirit has given the gift of joy to Christians facing the most terrible persecutions and humiliations in the Soviet Union, Poland, and elsewhere. In his book, *Risen Indeed: Lessons in Faith from the USSR*, Michael Bourdeaux, an Anglican priest, records the revival of faith in Russia among Russian Orthodox, Catholics, Pentecostals, Baptists, and others, notwithstanding decades of persecutions and restrictions on church activities.

"Suffering deepens and refines faith," writes Bourdeaux. "Out of it has come a joy and a commitment which Christians elsewhere so often lack."

Nijole Sadunaite, a young Lithuanian Catholic woman who devoted her life to nursing sick clergy and promoting the cause of freedom for the church, was sentenced in 1975 to six years' labor camp and exile for her religious activities. On hearing of her sentence, Nijole said, "How can I fail to be happy when Almighty God has already shown that light triumphs over darkness and truth over lies and falsehood?"

Nijole later wrote from a labor camp about a Russian Orthodox girl she had befriended: "Nadya Usoeva is a girl of remarkable goodness and tact [sentenced to seven years of strict-regime labor camp and two years exile]. She is a very decent and high-minded Russian Orthodox girl. We were like sisters. She was hardly ever permitted to 'take a holiday' at the labor camp. It is a real miracle: where does that fragile girl get her strength? Five years of punishment cell and strict-regime prison with hardly a break—starvation, cold and ridicule.

"She is a true heroine before whom we should all kneel. Quiet, calm, always smiling, with a prayer on her lips. I never heard her utter an impatient or rough word. She goes to the punishment cell smiling and returns smiling. Exhausted, blue with cold, she looks terrible, yet smiles not only at us, but at her tormentors as well."

Another modern Christian martyr unknown to the West, Sergei Iosifovich Fudel (1901–1977), the son of a Moscow priest, was imprisoned in 1921 for his church activities, and thereafter his life was a sequence of prison and exile sentences.

Still, he wrote in prison and in exile, without hope that his writings would ever be published; he wrote about the Russian Orthodox Church, its past and its future.

Fudel's memoirs finally were published by the underground Simizdat publication in Russia. This is an excerpt:

"The effect of Christian life always involves some kind of pain or suffering. But the suffering of a Christian life is like birth pains—they lead to joy. When we get embittered, when we grumble, it is always a danger sign. If we cannot be joyful, let us at least be good humored, but if not that, let us at least keep a sense of humor in our trials and temptations."

The same Spirit inspired Og Mandino to write in his book, *The Greatest Salesman in the World*: "I will laugh at the world. No living creature can laugh, except man and woman. If only I have the gift of laughter, it's mine to use whenever I choose. I will smile and my digestion will improve. I will chuckle and my burdens will be lightened. I will laugh and my life will be lengthened, for this is the great secret of long life. Most of all, I will laugh at myself, for mankind is most comical when he takes himself too seriously. . . . Never will I allow myself to become so important, so wise, so dignified, so powerful that I forget to laugh at myself and the world. In this matter, I will always remain as a child, for only as a child am I given the ability to look up to others."

Since 1964, that extraordinary Frenchman, Jean Vanier, has been busily establishing l'Arche communities for the mentally handicapped throughout the world. Vanier believes that "it is through every day life in community and the love which must be incarnate in this, that handicapped people can begin to discover that they have a value, that they are loved and so loveable."

In his book, *Community and Growth*, Vanier writes: "Forgiveness and celebration are at the heart of community. These are the two faces of love. . . . Our communities should be signs of joy and celebration. If they are, people will commit themselves with us. Communities which are sad are sterile; they are places of death. Of course our joy on earth is far from complete. But our celebrations are small signs of the eternal celebration, of the wedding feast to which we are all invited."

It is the same Spirit which gives a special flavor to the feast days and festivals honoring the many saints of the Roman Catholic and Orthodox churches. Down through the centuries, the Mediterranean Christians have been especially good at celebrating and are renowned for the effervescence of their festivals. A Greek festival overflows with joy, laughter, high humor, good food, lively music, singing, and circle dancing that excludes neither the young nor the old. It is both a religious event and a celebration of the joy of living.

A laugh is a prayer.

The Protestant Saints

Some Protestant sects have had the reputation of being so sour, cold, and judgmental that they were known as "God's frozen chosen." But I have known Catholics and Orthodox who fit that description, too. The Puritans have received the brunt of this criticism, not without some justification. H.L. Mencken, for instance, humorously defined Puritanism as "that haunting feeling that somewhere, some place, somebody is happy."

Some sects have taken pride in their long-faced gloominess and obsessive preoccupation with the Devil, evil, and hell. They have ignored the warning of Paul to the early Christians not to become preoccupied with evil but to keep their minds focused on what is good, beautiful, spiritually edifying, peaceful, and joyful.

Martin Luther was a good and pious man who, like all of us, was fallible. For instance, like a couple of popes, he ridiculed Copernicus's theory that the earth goes around the sun. Periodically throughout his life, when he was a celibate Catholic monk and also when he was a married Protestant reformer, Luther suffered from constipation and depressions. Music helped him handle his depressions, so he wrote a lot of beautiful hymns and songs. "Music is the greatest gift; indeed, it is divine," he wrote. "It puts to flight all sad thoughts. The Devil doesn't stay where there's music."

Luther also found it necessary, on occasion, to put the Devil to flight with laughter. Luther had a light side, and he enjoyed a hearty laugh. He and his wife, Katie, enjoyed inviting seminarians, students, and friends over for dinner, and Luther would regale them with stories and theology. There was much laughter at Luther's dinner table. Of course, there were jokes about Catholics made by Lutherans, and jokes about Lutherans by Catholics, and you laughed according to which side of the fence you were on.

Some of the students copied down Luther's discourses and pithy remarks at the dinner table, and they were eventually published under the title *Luther's Table Talks*.

He was appalled by the excesses of some of the reformers, of whom a friend wrote him: "So many sects arose among them that everybody was at sea, and none knew who was the cook and who the ladle."

"Good Lord!" Luther wrote. "Will our people at Wittenberg give wives even to monks? They will not push a wife on me." But when, years later, he unnerved the Catholics by marrying a former nun, Luther remarked of his wedding, "The angels laughed and the devils wept." And afterwards, he spoke often of the joys of marriage.

Luther could have a volcanic temper on occasion, but it was balanced by a sense of humor. Watching his dog eyeing a piece of meat, he commented, "If only I could pray the way that dog watches that morsel, all his thoughts concentrated on it!"

Once, while putting his young son to bed, Luther, who had studied law before becoming a monk, said, "If you become a lawyer, I will hang you on the gallows. It is almost impossible for lawyers to be saved. It's difficult enough for theologians."

Luther once lost his temper with a meticulous, overly virtuous exmonk who had joined his band. "For heaven's sake, why don't you go out and sin a little?" Luther told the exmonk. "God deserves to have something to forgive you for!"

No doubt Luther would have appreciated this story, which appeared not long ago in the newsletter of Trinity Lutheran Church in Battle Creek, Michigan:

"Visiting a neighborhood one afternoon, a pastor

knocked at the door of a church member but received no response. He was annoyed because he could hear footsteps and knew the mother of the family must be there.

"The pastor left his calling card, writing on it, 'Revelation 3:20. Behold I stand at the door and knock: if any man hear my voice and open the door, I will come in.'

"The next Sunday, as the parishioners filed out of the church after the service, the woman who had refused to answer the door greeted the pastor and handed him her card with Genesis 3:10 written on it. Later, the pastor looked up the passage: 'I heard thy voice in the garden, and I was afraid, because I was naked, and I hid myself.' "

Gloominess Is Not Holiness

Notions that holiness and gloominess were related spread into some of the religious movements of the seventeenth, eighteenth, and nineteenth centuries, and even spilled over into the present century.

John Wesley was a great preacher, a man with many admirable qualities. But he advised Methodist preachers that a preacher's "whole deportment before the congregation be serious, weighty, and solemn." Methodists were instructed in a discipline book to "be serious, let your motto be, holiness to the Lord. Avoid all lightness, jesting, and foolish talking."

But Wesley and other Methodist preachers were adept at using humor to put down hecklers and detractors. Wesley often rode on horseback to Methodist gatherings. A story says that one day on a narrow road he met an arrogant judge, also on horseback, coming in the other direction. The judge refused to budge, saying, "I shall not give the road to a fool."

"But I will," replied Wesley, calmly reining his horse off the road.

With a chuckle and a twinkle in his eye, a grand old retired Methodist minister told me that, after a careful reading of Wesley's life, he was convinced that the Methodist church would never have spread so fast had Wesley gotten along with his wife, a very difficult woman. He said Wesley was constantly taking to the road, preaching, as much to get away from his wife as to convert the wicked. She was, he said, Wesley's "thorn in the flesh."

Professor Doug Adams, chairman of the Christianity and Arts Department at Pacific School of Religion in Berkeley, California, has authored a delightful book called *Humor in the American Pulpit*, in which he chronicles the wit and humor of ninety-one leading American Protestant preachers in the eighteenth and nineteenth centuries. Adams says that the preachers used humor, jokes, and anecdotes "to help their people laugh in worship at American idolatries of power, wisdom, and wealth—idolatries that still attract our people's attention away from God."

Adams, a United Church of Christ minister, contends that religious scholars are partly at fault for representing eighteenth- and nineteenth-century American Christianity as humorless. Religious scholars, he said, either neglected or eliminated the humor in their subjects. The other possibility is that they didn't see it. Humorless scholars are not likely to see humor, any more than the blind can see the way to lead the blind. Adams, in his research, found humor—lots of it.

"In the East and on the frontier," observes Adams, "humor was used to gain a hearing; to attract and hold attention against all disruptions and to lead the people to hear and to accept the gospel with all of its controversial ideas and personal criticisms."

The churchmen directed their humor at the rich and the powerful, kings, presidents, politicians, the military, doc-

tors, professors, atheists, intellectuals, and—especially—
one another. The churchmen often combated one another's
theologies, or lack thereof, with humor.

Lyman Beecher, an early nineteenth-century preacher,
is credited with this prayer: "O Lord, grant that we may not
despise our rulers; and grant, O Lord, that they may not act
so we can't help it."

During the American Revolution, when British troops
forced a Boston minister to pray for King George at a worship service, the minister prayed, "O Lord, bless thy servant, King George, and grant unto him wisdom; for Thou
knowest, O Lord, he needs it."

Preachers of all denominations invariably had to deal
with hecklers, and humor was both a strategy and a defen-
sive shield. Lemuel Haynes, a black Congregationalist
preacher, once was confronted by two young men. "Have
you heard the good news?" one asked. "It's great news, and
if it is true, your business is done," the other said.

"What is it?" Haynes asked.

"The Devil is dead," said one.

The old preacher placed his hands on the heads of the
young men and said, "Poor fatherless children, what will
become of you?"

Treated with contempt in Boston by that city's traditional Christians, Jonathan Mayhew, an eighteenth-century
Congregational preacher, remarked wryly, "Whence comes
the doctrine that true orthodox Christians have a right to
persecute heretics and unbelievers? The Scripture teaches
us that those who will live godly in Christ Jesus must suffer
persecution; but not that they must persecute others." Needling certain pharisaical Christians who said but did not
do, Mayhew remarked, "They know their duty so exactly,

and believe it so firmly, that they imagine they may well be excused from doing it."

A lot of preachers then, as now, found amusing stories to tell about their parishioners, but the preachers themselves also were targets of jokes. In one nineteenth-century story, a man died and at his funeral the preacher delivered a long and seemingly endless sermon praising his virtues. The deceased was described as a good Christian and a pillar of the community, and he was praised for his generosity, faithfulness to his wife, and love for his children.

In the middle of the eulogy, the widow turned to one of her sons and said, "Son, you better go up to that coffin and see if that's your daddy in there."

Sam Jones, a late nineteenth-century Methodist preacher, was especially known for his wit, and he used humor to help get his gospel message across. It was Jones who said, "Some men open their mouths to laugh, and you can drop a great brickbat of truth right in."

Nineteenth-century preachers especially enjoyed needling the rich and intellectuals. "In most instances where nineteenth-century pulpit humor spoke of hell, the highly educated were pictured populating it," says Adams.

"Yes, there are plenty of brains in hell," Sam Jones remarked. "You understand that, don't you? What is culture worth if it is but the whitewash on a rascal? I would rather be in heaven learning my A.B.C.'s than sitting in hell reading Greek. We have been clamoring for forty years for a learned ministry and we have got it today, and the church is deader than it ever has been in history. Half of the literary preachers in this town are A.B.'s, Ph.D.'s, L.L.D's, and A.S.S.'s."

Reuben Tinker, a Presbyterian preacher in the 1830s–

40s, enjoyed needling the rich. "The heavier the purse hangs down, the tighter the strings," he said. He maintained that the poor almost always gave proportionately more than the rich, and that if a thousand people each were given a thousand dollars, they would give more than a rich man who was given a million dollars.

The Greatest Protestant Wit

The greatest Protestant wit of them all in the nineteenth century was Henry Ward Beecher, a Congregationalist whose preaching spanned the years 1837–1887. Beecher's ironic wit and humor flashed like lightning through his sermons.

"One of the best missionary influences vouchsafed to the human soul is wit and humor," Beecher said. "I throw out wit and humor and bring my hearers into a state of royal good nature, and through these elements, I bring in the truth which men do not like. Wit and humor [are] one of the most civilising of all the influences in the soul of man."

Beecher needled religionists who never did any wrong, but never did any good, either. "There are a great many people who seem to think religion means *not doing wrong*," he observed. "As if a knitting machine that never knit any stockings would be considered a good one because it never misknit! What is a man good for who simply does not do something?"

Beecher also needled end-times theologians who "study [the Book of] Revelation as they would a mathematical problem" and try to find "a Bonaparte in some he-goat," and who are so worried about what's going to happen tomorrow or five or one hundred years from now that they are unable to enjoy today and do the work of the Lord in the present. "Why, they might as well measure one of

Michelangelo's pictures by the square inch, and say it was better than Raphael's, because two feet larger; they might as well weigh their mother's love with a pair of steelyards."

He needled theologians, clergymen, and others who pretended they knew all the answers. "No one of these men rises up from his chair and says, 'We only know a little here and there of the great moral realm. We know things fragmentarily. We know only in part.' So said Paul; but then Paul would have had hard times in many modern churches."

He needled the pretensions of intellectuals: "As I recollect it, the God of Westminster Catechism ought not to be called Jehovah, but Analysis."

Adams notes that Beecher "used humor to encourage the people to take theology less seriously." "There stands a controversial dog at almost every turn," Beecher remarked. "And when you approach men on the subject of theology, this watchdog shows his teeth. Men call it 'conscience,' but a dog is a dog."

He needled the rich: "The creed of the greedy man is brief and consistent; and unlike other creeds, is both subscribed and believed. The chief end of man is to glorify *gold* and enjoy it forever: life is a time afforded man to grow rich in; death, the winding up of speculations; heaven, a mart of golden streets; hell, a place where shiftless men are punished with everlasting poverty."

The rich man, Beecher observed, becomes a slave to his money and possessions. "So they roll their possessions, as winter-boys in New England used to roll the snow. In rolling, it increases in magnitude, and it is at last vaster than they can shove. And when they have amassed it, what do they do? They let it stand where it is, and the summer finds it, and melts it away. It sinks to water again; and the water is sucked up, and goes to make snow once more for other foolish boys to roll into heaps."

In the 1870's, Beecher, referring to New York's millionaires and financial community, remarked: "The Kingdom of Heaven, to them, means the bank."

Adams tells me that he has since extended his study back to the early days of European Protestantism and has found a lot of humor there, too. A picture of John Calvin's solemnity has come down to us through the centuries, but Adams observes that Calvin, a lawyer, also had a light side. Adams said he unearthed some really witty remarks from Calvin's *Commentaries* on Scripture and from some of Calvin's sermons.

"Calvin once was talking about Biblical literalism and people who try to wrench meaning out of every word," Adams recalled, "and he flatly declared that a certain theologian was wrong and that 'anyone who wants to persist in this can go wiggle their ears!'"

The Disciples of Joy

In the early 1940s, American theologian Reinhold Niebuhr suggested that laughter was appropriate in the vestibule, but not in the sanctuary, of a church. "There is," Niebuhr said, "laughter in the vestibule of the temple, the echo of laughter in the temple itself, but only faith and prayer, and no laughter, in the holy of holies."

Niebuhr was a brilliant man, but his prophetic vision was clouded. The Pentecostal and charismatic movements have brought joy and laughter back into the sanctuary since Niebuhr wrote those words. The Pentecostal movement started in Topeka, Kansas, in 1901 under the guidance of Rev. Charles F. Parham, a Holiness preacher, and it has since spread phenomenally in the United States and elsewhere.

The charismatic movement springs from the Pentecostal movement, and it developed from the work of Rev. Dennis J. Bennett, an Episcopalian, in Van Nuys, California, in 1959. The charismatic movement has since spread to Catholic and Orthodox churches, and it is spreading like wildfire.

The trademark of the charismatic movement in all denominations has been a kind of defiant joy and celebration. Charismatics are sometimes called "the disciples of joy."

Some outsiders are baffled by the speaking and singing in tongues. But charismatic gatherings are marked not only by fervent prayer, but by a lot of joyous singing, hand clapping, foot stomping, touching, hugging, kissing, exclamations of joy, thanksgiving for healings, dancing—and laughter. Many, though not all, charismatics like to laugh, and they and their preachers often share some funny one-liners.

This is the kind of joke you may hear at a Protestant charismatic meeting.

A Congregational minister was visiting Georgia, and he went to a town where he found nothing but Pentecostal churches. Everywhere he went he found nothing but Pentecostals.

The minister walked into a Pentecostal church and told the preacher he was tired of meeting Pentecostals. He said he wanted to go some place where there weren't any Pentecostals.

The preacher replied, "Why don't you go to hell? There are no Pentecostals there."

Another Pentecostal preacher announced that the Holy Spirit had come upon him, convicted him, and told him to leave for Africa to be a missionary to the heathen.

"That wasn't the Holy Spirit," a woman in the audience shouted. "That was your ex-wife."

The Salvation Army has some Pentecostal features. Not long ago at a garage sale I found a very old Salvation Army bookmark with this advice: "Pray: it is the greatest power on earth. Love: it is a God-given privilege. Give: it is too short a day to be selfish. Work: it is the price of success. Play: it is the secret of perpetual youth. Laugh: it is the music of the soul."

Many other modern Protestant groups have had more than their share of fun-loving wits, clowns, and persons who have recognized and used the healing power of humor.

Since 1971, a Phoenix preacher, Rev. Dennis Daniel, pastor at Mountain View Baptist Church, has been drawing a cartoon called "Brother Blooper" for Baptist periodicals, poking fun at preachers and churches. Brother Blooper is a well-meaning but bumbling preacher who is always getting into hot water with his congregations and moving from church to church. He is chronically long-winded, and he is vexed when members of the congregation fall asleep or play miniature computer games during his sermons.

"We preachers tend to take ourselves and our churches too seriously," explained Rev. Daniel. "I sometimes catch myself being so serious that I turn people off. Christ should bring joy into our lives, and humor is an expression of that joy. The church is a very funny place. I can't think of any place funnier."

An hour before he was killed in a plane crash in Alabama in November 1983, Grady Nutt, a Baptist preacher who was known as "the prime minister of humor" on television's "Hee Haw," told a church audience, "An authentic response to life demands a chuckle as well as a boohoo. We're dang close, I think, in this era in our nation, to forgetting humor."

Not long ago, I heard the eminent Protestant minister, Elton Trueblood, give a speech to the Sun City, Arizona, Ministerial Association. Trueblood advised the clergymen: "Never trust a theologian who doesn't have a sense of humor."

In 1964, Trueblood wrote a perceptive little book called *The Humor of Christ*, which did not get the attention it deserved. Wrote Trueblood: "Anyone who reads the Synoptic Gospels with a relative freedom from presuppositions might be expected to see that Christ laughed, and that he expected others to laugh, but our capacity to miss this aspect of his life is phenomenal. We are so sure that he was always deadly serious that we often twist his words in order to make them conform to our preconceived mold. A misguided piety has made us fear that acceptance of his obvious wit and humor would somehow be mildly blasphemous or sacrilegious . . . The critics of Christ have, on the whole, been as blind to his humor as have his admirers."

Trueblood observed, "The consequences of Christ's rejection of the dismal are great, not only for common life, but also for theology. If Christ laughed a great deal, as the evidence shows, and if he is what he claimed to be, we cannot avoid the logical conclusion that there is laughter and gaiety in the heart of God."

Said Trueblood, "Any alleged Christianity which fails to express itself in gaiety, at some point, is clearly spurious. The Christian is gay, not because he is blind to injustice and suffering, but because he is convinced that these, in the light of the divine sovereignty, are never *ultimate*."

There is a revival of interest in humor as a healing force throughout all denominations. In view of the many different kinds of Christian humor and Christian expressions, one begins to suspect that God, though hating discord and disunity, loves variety—variety in humor, variety in worship.

In his book *Laughing Out Loud and Other Religious Experiences*, Tom Mullen, a Quaker, observes that "because Quakers are so serious about their religious concerns, they need a humorous perspective about themselves." Quakers have attacked major social problems and worked diligently for peace. "Fortunately," says Mullen, "some Friends have been able to keep perspective by laughing at themselves— even at their weightiest concerns.

"A long-standing Quaker joke illustrates the point. A Friend is awakened in the middle of the night to discover a burglar in the house. Quietly he gets his hunting rifle off the wall and confronts the thief. 'Friend robber," he says, 'I would not harm thee for the world, but thou standest where I am about to shoot!' "

Mullen added: "Religious people seldom laugh easily at their most deeply held convictions, because they do not want to demean these beliefs or deny their importance. The point, however, is this: an inability to laugh about our concerns too often results in idolatry of the cause. True Believers need the perspective humor provides. Otherwise, they become as self-righteous and unfunny as Luke's Pharisee. . . ."

A story is told that a junior high school class in a Texas church school was studying different Christian denominations. The teacher assigned students to write a brief composition on various religious groups. A boy handed in the following report on the Quakers: "Quakers are very peaceful people. They never fight or answer back. My father is a Quaker but my mother is not."

It is good to see some of the younger Protestant preachers showing a flair for humor and even using comedy to advantage. The dynamic young black television evangelist, Dr. Fred K. Price, of Inglewood, California, captivates audiences with preaching laced with earthy wit.

One of the funniest of the young Protestant evangelists is Mike Warnke, a very big man who has the talent either to wring howls of laughter from his audience or to bring them to a hushed silence as he delivers a serious message of salvation. His stories "Sergeant Klutzo Goes to Nam" and "Harpooned Hippo" in his album "Hey Doc!" are hilarious. In combat, pinned down by machine-gun fire and with artillery shells and aircraft bombs exploding all around him, Warnke actually got hit with an arrow from an enemy crossbow!

In his study of the humor of Protestant ministers, Professor Adams observed that "very few of the ministers studied attempted to stand above denominationalism. And even fewer succeeded in any attempt to give ecumenical perspective." An exception was George Whitefield, an eighteenth-century Anglican Methodist who came to America to preach to the colonies. "You see now, the sun shines on us all," Whitefield said. "I never heard that the sun said, 'Lord, I will not shine on Presbyterians; I will not shine on the Independents; I will not shine on the people called Methodists . . . or Papists.' "

The great Protestant preacher and healer Leslie Weatherhead maintained that belief is the door to joy. "The opposite of joy is not sorrow," Weatherhead said. "It is unbelief."

Whether a person brings upon himself joy or sorrow may depend on his or her image of Jesus.

"How do you picture God?" asks the Presbyterian minister, Rev. David Redding. "How about a God running toward you, arranging a celebration for you because he is crazy about you? I think this kind of God is behind Jesus' sense of humor. Did you ever think that one day you might run toward a God who would be running toward you, like the father who 'fell on his [prodigal] son's neck and kissed him'? "

PART III

In Search of Holy Images

Chapter 9

A HISTORY
OF HEALING IMAGES

The old saying that one picture is worth a thousand words may explain the remarkable staying power of sacred art and icons in the life of Christian churches down through the centuries. From the very earliest times, Christians have spread the gospel both by words and images.

Laurence of Ripafratta (1457) exhorted his monks to paint religious images and Biblical stories, saying, "The most persuasive tongue becomes silent in death, but your heavenly pictures will go on speaking of religion and virtue throughout the ages."

Religious wars have been fought over images. Christians who opposed images—iconoclasts—have persecuted Christians who venerated them—iconodules—and vice versa. But other Christians have used images as healing instruments. For centuries, up to the present time, many of the faithful have believed that holy images were instruments of the divine healing power and were even able to work miracles.

Orthodox and Roman Catholics are sometimes criticized for "praying to icons." They do not pray to icons; they pray before icons to whom they represent. The Seventh Ecumenical Council in 787, defending the veneration of icons, declared that "the honor rendered to the images goes to its prototype and the person who venerates an icon venerates the person represented on it. Such is the teaching of our holy fathers and the tradition of the Holy Catholic Church."

In the catacombs and elsewhere, the early Christians used the language of symbols to teach and inspire the faithful while confounding their pagan persecutors: a fish, a boat (symbol of the church), a lamb, the image of the Good Shepherd (Christ carrying a lamb on his shoulders or surrounded by sheep).

Surviving evidence indicates that early Christian art was generally positive and encouraging. Notwithstanding terrible persecutions, no scenes of martyrdom or persecution of the faithful—nothing negative or despairing—were depicted in the catacomb frescoes. Most of the symbolic primitive Christian art inspired faith and hope and pointed to the resurrection. As one historian of sacred art noted, "The pessimistic outlook of the pagan was replaced by the joyous confidence in the resurrection."

After the Emperor Constantine put an end to the Christian persecutions in the fourth century, churches and monasteries flourished, and so did sacred art, encouraged by the church fathers and monks. The eloquent Basil, for instance, after delivering a homily in praise of a martyr, urged painters to "rise now and let my words be surpassed by your painting of the heroic deeds of the martyr."

The word "icon" (eikon in Greek) translates into "image."

Paul described Christ as the "icon of the invisible god," and the church fathers maintained that the incarnation—the Word made flesh—justified the representation of Christ in art.

But it was the common folk who ardently sought an image of Christ. In his book, *Behold the Christ: A Portrayal of Christ in Words and Pictures*, Roland H. Bainton, an artist himself and one of the leading authorities on Martin Luther and the Protestant Reformation, observed, "One does not know how Jesus looked. No authentic likeness has come down to us. The New Testament gives us scarcely a hint . . . But successors did wish to know. The common people in particular desired a visible image, and it was they who initiated the impetus in Christian art."

But very soon, Christians fell to arguing fiercely with one another—a chronic, addictive, and self-destructive habit among Christians—as to how Christ should be represented in art, or whether he should be represented at all. In the eighth and ninth centuries, Christians, who had been instructed by Jesus to love and not to judge one another, fought bloody civil wars over images, and thousands upon thousands of icons and religious portraits were destroyed.

But if images carry the emotional power to make people mad enough to go to war, images also have been used to inspire and heal people.

At various times in Christian history—in the Mediterranean world and later in the Slavic countries and Russia—thousands upon thousands of icons and portraits of Christ and the saints were used not only in churches and monasteries, but also in homes and on roads. Many homes had an icon in every room. Many of these icons were credited with miraculous healings in the same way that the Eucharist, anointing with oil, the prayers of clergy and laypeople, and the knowledge and healing touch of a physician are instruments of God's healing power.

In Eastern Orthodox and Roman Catholic tradition, the identification of holy images with healing is firmly established. Many instances have been recorded of persons praying before icons, especially icons of Christ and Mary, and experiencing healings for themselves or loved ones. The icons themselves do not heal; it is Christ who heals through the saints and through the person praying. During the Lenten feast of "the Triumph of Orthodoxy" over iconoclasm in A.D. 843, the faithful bow before and kiss the icons, while a liturgical text is chanted declaring that the Holy Spirit, which inspired the image, "sanctifies the eyes of the faithful and heals both spiritual and corporeal diseases."

The First Icons Were Healing Images

A church tradition, shared by both Orthodox and Roman Catholics, says that the very first icons of Jesus were related to healing. One of the earliest representations of Jesus, according to that tradition, was a bronze statue reportedly erected in Caesarea Philippi by the hemorrhaging woman who was healed by Christ. The monument showed Jesus standing before a kneeling woman who entreats him with arms outstretched. The monument, destroyed in the fifth century by iconoclasts, was a forerunner of icons through which God was believed to work divine healing power.

According to another church tradition (some would prefer to call it a legend), the first icon of Christ, the "Holy Face," was made by Christ himself on a linen handkerchief, and this icon, too, is related to healing. This tradition has it that King Abgar the Black, a leper in the city of Edessa who had heard of Jesus "the good Physician," sent an artist named Hannan to do a portrait of Christ. But when Hannan saw Jesus, he was unable to do a portrait "because of the indescribable glory of his face."

Hannan asked Christ to go to Edessa and heal his king. Christ is said to have told the artist to tell the king, "Happy art thou who hast believed in me without having seen me, for it is written that they who see me shall not believe and they who do not see me shall believe." But he said he was about to return to the Father, and could not go to Edessa.

Christ washed and wiped his face with a linen handkerchief, and gave it to Hannan, the tradition holds. When King Abgar received the handkerchief, with the image of Christ fixed on it, he was healed of his leprosy and was converted.

The handkerchief was kept and venerated in Edessa until the mid-tenth century, when it was taken to Constantinople. It was lost when the Crusaders sacked Constantinople in 1204.

In the Orthodox Church, the handkerchief Holy Face became the prototype for all the representations of Jesus for fifteen centuries. Thousands of copies and versions of the Holy Face, based on the handkerchief prototype, were reproduced and hung in churches and homes. The Orthodox Church established strict guidelines and rules for iconographers and did not allow them to deviate from the essence of this prototype, to portray Jesus according to the imagination of the artist, or to use human models.

The Roman Catholic Church also venerates the Holy Face but in the last thousand years or so has tolerated a wider variety of representations of Christ by artists, as have the Protestant churches.

Some theologians question the authenticity of the Holy Face image and argue that it cannot be verified. It is not my intention to enter a theological argument over these images. I love the icons of the Orthodox Church, but I also love many of the portraits of Jesus done by Roman Catholic and Protestant artists.

"Christ the Teacher" Orthodox icon.

"Jesus Healing a Leper"
by Karl Thylmann.

Icon of St. Eustratios healing a demoniac.

"Madonna of the Ros
with smiling Christ chi
by Rapha

Crucified Christ comforting
St. Bernard.

There is a certain severity to the face of Christ depicted in a twelfth-century icon of the Holy Face. This is clearly Christ the Judge, and he is represented in this way at a time when the Moslems are threatening both Orthodox Byzantium and Catholic lands, the Crusaders are locked in battle with the Moslems, and even the Christians are fighting among themselves. In the midst of all this bloodshed, carnage, and chaos, the artist seems to be sending a message to the rulers of this world and mortal men and women that Christ reigns notwithstanding and is the final judge of all.

Every year on August 16, the Orthodox Church celebrates the Feast of the Holy Face. The faithful make the sign of the cross before this icon (or one very similar to it), bow, and kiss it. This liturgical text is sung: "We venerate Thy most pure image, by which Thou has saved us from the servitude of the enemy. By representation, Thou healest our diseases."

I found a more modern representation of the Holy Face, an icon called "Christ the Teacher" in a Russian Orthodox church in Battle Creek, Michigan. One of my favorites, it reflects, in my opinion, the best of Orthodox spirituality in iconography—both divine power and divine gentleness.

An icon of the Holy Face, perhaps very similar to this one, inspired St. John of Damascus (675–749) to write, "I saw the human image of God and my soul was saved." He then became one of the chief champions of icons.

An old (fourteenth-century or earlier) Byzantine icon of the Holy Mother and the Christ Child also is believed to have worked many healing miracles. The icon was found undamaged after a church in the village of Reehanya, Lebanon, burned down in 1554. The people called the icon "The Burning Bush." When plague struck the area, killing many people, the clergy carried the icon in a procession through contaminated areas. The epidemic is said to have come to an end wherever the icon passed, and the people gave it another name: "The Healer."

In 1939, the icon was transferred and carried into the Church of Gethsemane. A priest who was very weak and critically ill with stomach cancer was praying at a service. Suddenly, the priest turned around and said in a loud voice, "This icon is truly miraculous. A certain power is emanating from it. I feel this power. I am no longer ill." He lived another ten years.

The Icons of Physicians Venerated

The Orthodox and Catholic faithful also venerated the icons of physicians and other healers who were canonized. Foremost among these physician-saints were St. Cosmas and St. Damian, who are called "the Unmercenary Healers" because they never took money from their patients. Their enemies finally fed them to the sharks.

Cosmas and Damian were Greek brothers who studied medicine in the Hippocratic schools of the third century. They are reputed to have healed their patients with herbs and prayer, especially prayer to the Holy Mother. They are said to have cured all kinds of illnesses, but they believed that their patients were cured by the grace of God.

Another Greek physician, St. Panteleimon, is venerated as the patron saint of physicians. St. Panteleimon is often shown holding medical instruments and ointments. A physician to Emperor Maximian, he was converted by a Christian priest, and he dedicated his skills in healing to Christ. When still a young man, he was denounced to the emperor as a believer in Christ, arrested, and executed by the sword in A.D. 305.

Devotion to the martyred Panteleimon spread far and wide in the early church. In A.D. 532, Justinian I rebuilt a church that had been dedicated to him at an earlier date.

A couple of very old icons depicting the miracles of St. Eustratios have survived in St. Catherine's Monastery on Mount Sinai. One icon shows St. Eustratios healing a demoniac, or what the psychiatrists of today would diagnose as a psychotic, schizophrenic, or manic-depressive. In this icon, a clergyman stands at the right carrying a box containing the relics of St. Eustratios, an indication that the healing of the demoniac took place *after* the saint's death, and his presence is being invoked through prayer by the clergyman and his two companions.

"Christian healing is not a fad of the twentieth century," *The Orthodox Weekly Bulletin* observed recently. "Great Christian healers were known in the church in ancient times, and their loving sacrifice on behalf of the sick has been an inspiration for many." Some of them were— like Christ—martyred.

Depictions of Jesus Varied Widely

The representations of Jesus himself—the Great Physician, the Divine Healer—have varied widely down through the centuries. Artists have seen Jesus differently, through eyes colored by their religious, cultural, ethnic, national, and political perspectives. And perhaps even the emotional makeup of the artist has influenced his or her perception of Jesus. Many artists clearly have identified with the "man of sorrows" and with the pain of the crucified Christ. They have projected their own emotional and spiritual pain onto the image of Jesus.

Roland Bainton observes that "some artists have sought

to be faithful to history by putting the entire life of Christ in a Palestinian setting. However, the majority of artists have transferred Palestine to their own countries, using local colors, costumes, and faces. Thus to universalize Christ is legitimate . . . Jesus may be given a face that is brown, white, black, or yellow . . ."

I have pored over many collections of sacred art, including Bainton's, going back fifteen centuries prior to the twentieth century, and nowhere have I been able to find a representation of a smiling or laughing Jesus, or at least, an adult smiling Christ. A well-known Eastern Orthodox educator, Professor Charles Ashanin, of the Christian Theological Seminary (a Protestant institution in Indianapolis), tells me he has never seen an icon of a smiling, laughing, or joyful Jesus.

The only evidence (and very dubious it is) that Christ did not laugh is contained in a letter purportedly written by Publius Lentulus, a Roman official in Judea and supposedly a friend of Pontius Pilate, to the Roman Senate of the first century. The letter describes Christ as "a man of noble and well-proportioned stature, with a face full of kindness and firmness, so that the beholders both love him and fear him. His hair is the color of wine and golden at the root . . . and divided down the center after the fashion of the Nazarenes. His beard is full. His eyes blue and extremely brilliant. In reproof and rebuke, he is formidable; in exhortation and teaching, gentle and amiable of tongue. None have seen him to laugh, but many on the contrary to weep. . . ." Some scholars suspect the Lentulus letter is a forgery written several centuries after Christ.

Only a few artists before our time have dared to put the hint of a smile on the lips of the Christ child. You can see a trace of a smile on the infant Jesus in the painting by Raphael called "Madonna of the Rose."

One of Rome's holiest icons, La Madonna della Clemenza, dates back to the seventh or eighth centuries, when Greek popes attempted to unify the Church to confront Moslem invasions and iconoclastic challenges. The Virgin is flanked by two archangels, and a youthful Jesus sits on her lap. All of the faces reflect peace and serenity. The icon has been damaged, but there appears to be a boyish smile on the young Jesus' face.

Even those few artists who found a trace of joy in the face of the infant Jesus never saw it in the face of the adult Jesus. One searches in vain for a joyful Christ, and one cannot even find him in the depictions of the most triumphant and joyous occasions in his life—the joyous entry into Jerusalem on Palm Sunday, the transfiguration, when "his face shone like the sun" (Matt. 17:1–3), and the resurrection with its victory over death.

An authority on icons, Richard Temple, author of *Icons: A Search for Inner Meaning*, observes that "when we enter the world of icons . . . we enter a world of the inward spirit: the mystical world of spiritual realities rather than the world of ordinary physical realities. It is a world inhabited by angels, by saints, by the Mother of God, and by Jesus Himself. In our world, there is darkness and confusion; in the icons, there is only light, harmony, and order."

The monk-iconographers practiced the spiritual and physical disciplines of "hesychasm" ("hesychia" means "quiet"), and they strove to reflect that inner quiet and serenity in their paintings. While painting an icon, an Orthodox monk would repeatedly say to himself the Jesus Prayer, the prayer of the heart: "Jesus Christ, Son of God, have mercy on me, a sinner." He would practice breathing exercises similar to yoga; fast, eat sparingly a vegetarian diet, do physical labor, and partake of the Eucharist. He would, in effect, fast from earthly distractions to the mind.

"During all this," Temple observes, "he [the monk] may know moments or periods of joy and may experience his soul bathed in warmth and light, but he must not allow this to distract him."

Are Saintly Faces Bright or Dark?

A section of the Orthodox Church liturgy on the Feast of the Holy Face, commemorating the transfiguration of Christ, declares, "Falling to the ground on the holy mountain, the greatest of the apostles prostrated themselves upon seeing the Lord reveal the dawn of a divine brightness, and now we prostrate ourselves before the Holy Face which shines forth brighter than the sun."

There is no detailed account of how Jesus' face looked to his disciples, Peter, James and John, when he was transfigured on the mountain. All we have is the spare account that "there in their presence he was transfigured: his face shone like the sun and his clothes became as white as the light" (Matt. 17:1–3).

Much later, Prince Abgar's emissary was not able to paint a portrait of Jesus "because of the indescribable glory of his face which was changing through grace."

One would suppose that a face shining like the sun would not be reflecting darkness or sorrow or despair or judgmental anger; rather, that face would be reflecting warmth and love and calmness and joy—the attributes of God. It would be a happy face. Folklore has always related happiness and sunshine.

A seventeenth-century Russian iconographer, Joseph Vladimirov, who was an admirer of Western art, once challenged some of the Orthodox Church's strictures on the painting of icons, especially the portrayal of Jesus and the saints with darkened faces of a metallic brownish color.

"Where," Vladimirov asked one archdeacon who was a traditional iconographer, "can one find a rule which says that the faces of the saints must all be represented equally bronzed and darkened? All of the saints did not have thin and dark faces. And if certain saints, during their life, did not have a healthy appearance because they neglected their bodies, then after their death, having received the crown of the just, they must have changed their appearance to a lighter aspect because a bright countenance befits the just, and a dark one, the sinners. But many saints were distinguishable by an amazing beauty even during their lifetime. Must they, too, be represented with darkened faces?

"When the great prophet Moses received the law on Mount Sinai from the Lord, then the children of Israel could not look at Moses' face because of the brightness which rested on him. Must the faces of Moses also be represented bronzed and dark the way that you do? In our time you expect iconographers to paint dark images which do not resemble the beauty of their prototypes, and you teach us to lie against the ancient Scriptures."*

In turn, Leonide Ouspensky, author of *Theology of the Icon* and one of the foremost authorities on icons, argues that there is no way for an artist to depict a face which "shines brighter than the sun" with colors or form, except symbolically with a halo. He insists that "the icon must correspond to sacred texts which are absolutely explicit."

Bainton notes that "the piety of the Cistercians and

---

*From Leonide Ouspensky, *Theology of the Icon*. (See Bibliography for complete reference information.)

Franciscans introduced a different style. Both stressed the infinite love and tenderness of Christ."

A Cistercian depiction of Christ as judge shows him with his feet on a honeycomb, a reference to St. Bernard's remark: "Christ is my bee. He comes not to sting, but to bring me honey."

Another Cistercian work shows Christ, nailed to the cross by his feet only, stretching out his arms to embrace St. Bernard.

But again, there are no known representations of a smiling Christ even among the early Franciscans and Cistercians, who stressed following the Lord in peace, compassion, and joy.

The traditional Orthodox Catholic view of the icon is tied into the belief that man and woman are created in the image and likeness of God, and that every person is an icon. The divine image was tainted, in this view, by the fall of Adam, but the grace of baptism restores the image of God to humanity. Thereafter, like a painter, God works at outlining the divine likeness in the individual, who must put forth spiritual effort to acquire the virtues of the divine likeness—love and joy.

If so many scriptural and liturgical passages are filled with references to joy, gladness, or rejoicing, and if there is every indication that Jesus himself reflected not only great light, but also great joy and even humor, why until very recently were there no representations of a joyful Jesus or happy saints?

The Iconoclastic Wars

Even in the early centuries of Christianity there were strong iconoclastic trends among both Christians and Jews, who regarded images of any kind as idolatrous. Any representations of a joyful Jesus, along with those of a sorrowful Jesus, could well have been destroyed by Christian, Jewish, and pagan iconoclasts of the earlier centuries.

Icons and sacred art flourished in the centuries following Constantine, but in the West, invading barbarians destroyed much sacred art, and to the East the iconoclastic Moslems destroyed much Byzantine art. In 723, the Moslem Caliph ordered icons removed from all Christian churches in lands under his rule.

But if there were any chance of a joyful Jesus surviving the onslaughts of pagan, Jewish, and Moslem iconoclasts, the Christian iconoclasts themselves administered the coup de grace in the eighth and ninth centuries.

It is difficult, from this distance, to comprehend the depth and intensity of the rage of the iconoclasts against images. The iconoclasts accused the iconodules of idolatry, insisting that it was impossible to portray in painting both the divine and human natures of Christ.

The iconoclasts were apparently responding to abuses and excesses in the veneration of icons. Some Christians decorated their clothing with holy images. Some priests allowed icons to be used as substitutes for godparents at baptism. Other Christians misunderstood the function of the icon and would venerate the image itself instead of the person represented on the image. Still other Christians came to believe that the veneration of icons alone would ensure their salvation.

Yet, many of the iconoclasts, who were violently opposed to holy images, were not reluctant to have their own portraits painted and distributed around town. One of the champions of holy images, Methodius I, patriarch of Constantinople (847), was cruelly persecuted and reduced to a skeleton by the iconoclastic emperor Theophilus. Theophilus summoned the feisty patriarch and demanded that he cease the veneration of holy images. Methodius replied, "If an image is so worthless in your eyes, how is it that when you condemn the images of Christ, you do not also condemn the veneration paid to representations of yourself? Far from doing so, you are continually causing them to multiply."

The iconoclasts persecuted, tortured, excommunicated, and executed the iconodules. They burned the hands of monk-iconographers, confiscated their properties, and destroyed thousands of works of sacred art. The iconodules, when they returned to power, retaliated in kind, excommunicating and severely persecuting the iconoclasts. Both sides regarded the other as heretics. During this period, emperors, patriarchs, and bishops rose to power and fell according to whether they favored or opposed holy images.

Ouspensky describes the end result of the iconoclastic period: "Everything that could be destroyed was destroyed. Images were subjected to every possible outrage. They were broken, burned, and painted over. The mosaics were torn down. Civil servants were sent to the most distant provinces to search out and destroy the works of sacred art. Everything beautiful disappeared from the churches."

A representation of a joyful Jesus would have had little chance of surviving this mass destruction.

As a result of the iconoclastic period, Ouspensky admits, "we can no longer say what icons from early Christian times were like."

The iconoclastic period had a far-reaching effect on Christendom and the Byzantine Empire. It resulted in the exile and emigration of about fifty thousand Orthodox monks to Italy and the closing of many monasteries. The seemingly endless religious wars between the Christian iconoclasts and the Christian iconodules divided the Byzantine Empire, sapped its energies, killed its citizens, and made it an easy prey for the invading Moslems, who eventually took over Constantinople. The Moslems, rejoicing in the divisions among the Christians, swept in and conquered both the Christian iconoclasts and the Christian iconodules. The result was that Christians had great difficulty worshiping with or without images, and many of them found it practical to become Moslems.

On the first Sunday of Lent, the Orthodox Church worldwide annually celebrates the "Feast of the Triumph of Orthodoxy" over iconoclasm in 843, when the veneration of icons was reestablished in the church. But if in fact it was a triumph, it was a short-lived one. The iconoclastic dispute was a major factor in wrecking the Byzantine Empire, making it easy prey for the Moslems.

Herein, perhaps, lies an ecumenical lesson. The principle is a simple one: divided Christians who attack one another sooner or later are swallowed up by their non-Christian adversaries.

After the veneration of icons was reestablished in 843, the Orthodox Church, in an effort to correct abuses, laid down strict regulations for icon artists which prevented them from exercising their imaginations in portraying Jesus.

Consider, too, that many of the iconographers were monks who were living in fear of persecution, torture, exile, or death. It was not usual for these artists, as they sat before their easels, to imagine a smiling or joyful Jesus. More likely, iconographers would identify with the sorrowful, crucified Jesus, or with the Jesus of judgment who eventually would dispatch their persecutors to everlasting hellfire.

For the past thousand years, there have been successive waves of iconoclastic rage resulting in the destruction and looting of thousands of works of art: the sacking of Constantinople by the Crusaders, the iconoclastic excesses of the Turks who conquered much of the Byzantine Empire, the iconoclasm of some Protestant groups, the destruction and looting of churches and sacred art by the Nazis and Communists in this century.

I suspect that the iconoclasts of all periods would have had a special dislike for an image of a smiling Christ; and I suspect that if they came across an image of a joyful Jesus, they would be quick to destroy it, just as many were eager to crucify him when he joyfully walked this earth in the flesh.

The sight of happiness in others has always annoyed and angered certain kinds of people. There is an altogether human tendency among the unhappy to be jealous and resentful of people who are happy. Some people who are in pain also are inclined to want to inflict pain on others. They would be in the forefront of those who wanted to crucify Jesus.

These people cannot tolerate joy or humor. They are people who nurse their hatreds and find it impossible to forgive. They are obsessed with evil, reject beauty, and seek neither love nor peace. They are always with us.

Bainton observed that "the view that the corporeal is not a fit vehicle for the divine leads to a rejection of music through the ear, pictures through the eye, and sacraments through the mouth. The view that the flesh is the garment rather than the tomb of the spirit allows for the musical, artistic, and sacramental, with room for variety of emphasis."

All of these reasons may have contributed to the lack of representations of a joyful Jesus in traditional religious art.

Jesus Has Many Faces

"The writers of the New Testament," Bainton observed, "were interested in what Jesus said and did rather than in how he looked. Perhaps this is all to the good, because it means that each period and people has been free to envision him in its own way. The diverse pictures are not false. Each has seized upon some valid feature. The variety attests to Christ's universality. However, there may be distortions, and any depiction which excludes the others is to that degree false.

"Every age and every clime has found in him that which has spoken to its condition. They were all right. What they depicted was true, but distorted because partial. And to a degree they were misleading, because to make Christ just like one of ourselves is to obscure his greatness. Yet, one is reminded of what happened when the Turks took Constantinople and plastered over the mosaics of Christ. With the centuries, the plaster has cracked and the image of Christ shows through."

Jesus has many faces. You can see him in the faces of children, (". . . for it is to such as these that the kingdom of heaven belongs" Matt. 14:15).

You can see him in the faces of the poor, the lonely, the imprisoned. "For I was hungry and you gave me food; I was thirsty and you gave me drink; I was a stranger and you made me welcome; naked and you clothed me; sick and you visited me; in prison and you came to see me," Jesus told his disciples. And the disciples asked: "Lord, when did we see you hungry and feed you; or thirsty and give you drink? When did we see you a stranger and make you welcome; naked and clothe you; sick or in prison and go to see you?"

And Jesus answered, "I tell you solemnly, in so far as

you did this to one of the least of these brothers of mine, you did it to me" (Matt. 25:35–40).

I believe we should honor all representations of Jesus, but it is bothersome that so many artists down through the centuries have been obsessed with portraying Jesus' sorrowful side, to the exclusion of his joyful side. There is an old Mediterranean proverb that "all the world is a mirror and gives back to every man [or woman] the reflection of his [or her] own face." Have many of these artists been giving us the reflections of their own faces?

Sometimes I feel uncomfortable with portrayals of Jesus—who repeatedly criticized the judgmental Pharisees and lawyers, who was himself quick to forgive, and who advised his disciples: "Judge not that ye be not judged"—as a harsh judge himself. But I am not about to argue with anyone who sees Christ as a judge.

Nor will I take issue with those who see the clown as a symbol of Christ. St. Paul says that we must all be "fools for Christ."

I personally visualize Jesus as the best of friends, who weeps with us when we weep and laughs with us when we laugh. I believe that at a time when the public is being bombarded by negative, violent, and sick images through television and other media, we greatly need the image of a joyful Jesus. And I believe that the day of the smiling Christ has come upon us.

A young clergyman told me recently, "We have lost the main message of Christianity—that suffering leads to joy—and we must recapture it."

Chapter 10

MODERN IMAGES
OF JOY AND LAUGHTER

When an article I wrote entitled "Jesus Put on a Happy Face" appeared in the September 1983 issue of *St. Anthony Messenger*, it precipitated a strong and mostly positive reader response. Franciscan Father Jack Wintz, associate editor, commented, "Quite a few letters have been coming to us, proving that your theme [of a laughing, joyful, fun-loving Jesus] has a strong resonance in the popular mind and heart."

I had mentioned in the article that we were collecting, where we can find them, paintings and drawings of smiling and laughing Christs, but that they were hard to find, and that we had located only four so far. *St. Anthony Messenger* readers and others responded by sending us various artists' representations of smiling and laughing Christs. (Comedian Steve Allen responded by sending me, at Christmas, a photograph of himself smiling, signed: "To Cal—Best Wishes, Steve Allen.")

Some of the paintings and drawings were done by Catholic artists, and others by Protestants. Many of the readers reported that they had had great difficulty finding paintings or drawings of a smiling Christ and wanted to know where they could buy one.

"Christ: the Essence of Life, Light, Love and Laughter" by Joyce Martin. © Spes in Deo Publications, 1979.

"Smiling Christ" by Lawrence Zink. © Lawrence Zink, St. Anthony Messenger Magazine.

"Smiling Christ" by Frances Hook. © John Brandi Co., Inc.

'Jesus Laughing," a color screen-print adaptation by Ralph Kozak of an original drawing by Willis Wheatley. Canadian copyright, Willis Wheatley; U.S. copyright, Ralph Kozak.

"My Friend." Smiling Christ with young girl, by Frances Hook. © Apostleship of Prayer, 1979.

"Smiling Christ" by John Steel. © Providence Lithograph Co., 1981.

"The Black Christ." 1984 icon by Robert Lentz.

Almost without exception, those correspondents who sent us portrayals they had found reported that the joyful images of the Son of God were inspiring, cheering, hopeful, and reassuring in these troubled times.

The most touching letter came from an eighty-four-year-old woman dying of cancer in a Billings, Montana, hospital. Gretchen J. Heupel offered to send us a photograph of a smiling Christ painting that she had hanging in her apartment since the early 1940s. At that time she had cut out and framed a painting of a smiling Christ seated on a mound, with three small children gathered around him, that had appeared on the cover of *Extension* magazine in Chicago. Heupel said she planned to give the framed picture to her cousin for photographing. "But," Miss Heupel wrote, "my cousin couldn't bear to take it down while I'm still alive, so you will have to wait, I guess, for my death— any time God chooses. I'm as ready for death as I'll ever be, for a long time now, so all I ask is a prayer." She died shortly after writing this letter, and a relative sent us the smiling Christ that Gretchen Heupel cherished and that helped sustain her for so many years.

JoAnn Marciszewski of the Catholic Church Extension Society in Chicago identified the artist of Heupel's painting as W. C. Griffith, who prepared it for the cover of the August 1942 issue of *Extension* magazine. The painting received such a positive response from readers that many prints were sold; the original, however, has since disappeared, and prints are no longer available.

Interestingly, Griffith did this bright and hopeful painting during a very dark period in American history—not long after Pearl Harbor, when Americans were at war on several fronts.

She Saw Christ in the Faces of Her Family

Joyce Martin is an effervescent mother of seven and grandmother of sixteen who, with her husband Peter, organized Spes in Deo, a Franciscan Family Retreat in Montrose, Colorado. Martin also is a painter, and for years she was puzzled because, growing up as a Roman Catholic, she had never seen a painting or representation of a smiling or laughing Christ. So, a few years ago, she herself set out to paint a happy Christ.

"In studying church history, it seems to me our ancestors, from the middle of the second hundred years after Christ, got off the track with the Christian message and have been concentrating on the negative ever since, except for a few joyous souls along the way," Martin told me. "They stand out like radiant lights every so often across the centuries. St. Francis was one of the most joyful; yet in his joy, he certainly was inspired to weep. However, God loves each of us in equal measure, be we fools and jesters or weepers and hand-wringers.

"When we arrive at that kind of balance where we are paradoxically the saint who can both weep and dance with joy, we begin to understand more fully the meaning of the gospel story. We should be both joyful and yet have the sadness in our heart that feels the plight of our suffering brother and be able to suffer with him."

Mrs. Martin commented, "I think we have had it all wrong for centuries; Christ had a happy life. It was his joy that attracted others to him; his suffering and death were only a very small fraction of what his life was all about. Too long we have lived and acted the fraction of his life, instead of bringing his joy, love, peace, and hope to the world. No wonder as Christians we have failed. We have had nothing to offer the suffering world but a message of more suffering."

It took five years for Martin to complete her smiling Christ. She had trouble finding a suitable model. "Finally," she recalls, "one evening my husband Peter was sitting beside me on the couch with several of the children sitting around on the floor. Their dad was leading us in the rosary. I looked at his face in repose, with all its gentleness, love, and humility, and I heard within my being: 'Here is your Christ.' 'God,' I thought, 'you have got to be kidding! A bald-headed Christ?' "

Mrs. Martin's painting turned out to be a composite of her husband, her sons, and her daughters. "And, yes, I guess that is how I see Christ—in the happiness of the members of my family," she said. "I hope that love will grow to the extent that I can see Christ in all the others whose lives touch mine. I am not at the second stage by a long shot yet!"

Martin titled her painting: "Christ: The Essence of Life, Light, Love, and Laughter."

The Smiling Christ of Cincinnati

The editors of *St. Anthony Messenger* commissioned their own gifted art director, Lawrence Zink, to paint his version of a smiling Christ to illustrate my article. I asked Zink, who lives in Cincinnati, whether he used the neighborhood Greek, Italian, Lebanese, or Jewish boy as a model. "Actually," Zink said, "the model was my son, Larry, who is neither Greek, Italian, Lebanese, or Jewish. But I'm glad some of those characteristics showed through."

It's intriguing that Zink, like Martin, also chose a member of his family as a model. Is it possible that we invariably see Jesus in those people that we love most? But is it also possible that Jesus is in the strangers we meet, and we have trouble seeing him in strangers because we are stingy with our love?

The magazine received many requests from readers for reprints of the Zink painting. Gertrude Robb of Chicago wrote, "For many years, I have tried to find a painting which was called the laughing Christ, and have been told many times that there is no such painting. I am especially eager to find a print suitable for framing."

Anne M. Fox of Philadelphia wrote asking for a print of the Zink painting. "I belong to a prayer group," she said, "and was really concerned when some people told me they could not even imagine Christ smiling, even in their most quiet moment. I thought if I could obtain the picture, it might help them to see Jesus in another light."

Loretta G. Doneete of East Falmouth, Massachusetts, wrote that she and two members of her prayer group loved the painting. "I belong to a charismatic prayer group," she wrote, "and for the past two months we have had prophecies of repentance and warnings of God's punishment. Even on the night of praise, the warnings, full of doom, still came and they sure put me on edge. The last meeting I went to I prayed for the Holy Spirit to help me discern and give me some message to bring God's joy. He did, and I let it all spill out. To this day, I cannot tell you my exact words but it was entirely a message of joy. Mr. Samra's article was a confirmation, and I have been thanking and praising God ever since. Thank you for publishing this wonderful piece of joy.

"How could Jesus ever attract children and disciples if he never smiled or enjoyed people? Jesus is a joyous God

and wants us to be joyful. It brings to my mind a verse by
Ella Wheeler Wilcox:

> Laugh and the world laughs with you;
> Weep and you weep alone,
> It's a sad old earth that must borrow its mirth,
> It has trouble enough of its own.

Greg Bradt of Northboro, Massachusetts, wrote,
"Throughout my life, whenever I have tried to bring forth a
mental picture of Jesus, he never seemed happy. Always
grim or sad. I feel it can only be uplifting and inspirational
for people to see the happiness and joy of Jesus Christ. If
you could send me a picture of a happy Jesus, I would be
grateful."

Wrote Mary L. Fulmer of Newport, Kentucky:
"Wouldn't it be wonderful if every home had a picture of
the smiling Jesus? As the mother of five and the grandmother of four, I have looked to my picture of the Sacred
Heart of Jesus to ease my pain and sorrow. But Jesus always
looks so sad. I just think it would be a wonderful experience
to have both pictures side by side to show all of us that sorrow and sadness can become love and happiness if we believe in him who loves us."

Elisa A. Pisani of Astoria, New York, wrote, "This may
sound silly, but when I saw the title 'Laughing Jesus,' I
couldn't help but laugh. Whenever I look at a picture of Jesus, I always think he is smiling."

Justus H. Herman of Fort Lauderdale, Florida, sent
along a Father's Day greeting card with a smiling Christ
holding a young boy, sent to him by his daughter. He wrote,
"For a number of years I have been looking for a picture of
Jesus smiling. In fact, I have discussed this with friends,
and many have said they had never thought of this. I was

thrilled with your article, which makes me feel much better knowing that I am not the only one seeking the smiling Jesus."

Esther L. Klinke of Amarillo, Texas, reported that she has "a beautiful picture of a smiling Christ by the late Ivan Pusecker which has been in the family for years. The picture is a great inspiration and consoling force for my family.

"I love the sorrowful Jesus, too, but am certain that the resurrected Jesus had to be a very happy man! Recently, we placed a monument on our rural cemetery with just the head of Christ engraved into the marble. At our request, the artist has just a semblance of a smile on Christ's face; to us, it is beautiful and reassuring."

The Laughing Christs of Traverse City and Toronto

The drawing titled "The Laughing Christ" that I first encountered at the Franciscan Renewal Center in Scottsdale, Arizona was done anonymously, and it took me almost three years to track down the artist. That drawing, we learned, was being produced and sold by the Paulist Fathers at Old St. Mary's Church in San Francisco.

In Kalamazoo we found a similar representation titled "Jesus Laughing," a color screen-print distributed by Praise Screen Prints and Ralph Kozak, of Traverse City, Michigan. Kozak is a congenial, 59-year-old charismatic Catholic and sign painter by trade. I felt a rather special accord with him, perhaps because both of us had come to Jesus fully rather late in life.

Kozak told me the drawing conveyed the sense of joy he felt after being baptized in the Spirit. He said he, too, had wondered who had drawn it, and had heard that the artist was a convict. Kozak said he changed the drawing somewhat, added color, called it "Jesus Laughing," took out a U.S. copyright, and with his wife and children launched a ministry focused entirely on distributing color screen prints and shirts showing Jesus laughing.

A nun in California finally identified the original artist as Willis Wheatley of Toronto, who was a Canadian Protestant but not a convict. Wheatley, who died in 1984, was the head of the art department of the United Church of Canada, a union of Presbyterians, Methodists, and Congregationalists.

According to Dr. Gordon Freer, the United Church of Canada commissioned Wheatley to do the drawing in charcoal under the title "Jesus Christ—Liberator" for a youth program in 1973. Freer said "the drawing's popularity was phenomenal, and we began to see copies appearing all over the world." Mr. and Mrs. Wheatley, who owned the Canadian copyright, were generous and allowed the reproductions, he said.

Somewhere in heaven, Willis Wheatley, the Canadian Protestant, must be greatly amused that his drawing of a God of joy and laughter has found a home with so many American Catholics.

The Visions of Other Artists

The Providence Lithograph Company of Rhode Island not long ago commissioned a gifted artist, John Steel, to do a painting called "The Smiling Christ." "This painting was done for us to show the love and friendship Christ had for his followers," according to Kenneth J. Hoyt, religious sales manager. Steel's portrayal has gained many admirers.

One of my favorite portrayals of Jesus is a painting by the very talented Frances Hook. Hers is a rather brawny Jesus with a huge, warm, friendly smile on his face. He is fearless and very approachable.

Pat Ryan of the Bronx, New York, gifted us with three other magnificent paintings of smiling Christs by Frances Hook: "My Friend," showing Christ with a young girl; "The Listener," Christ with a young boy; and "Our Brother," Christ with four children. According to Father F. J. Power, Richard Hook, before he died, taught Frances Hook how to paint in his style and with his technique. She died in 1983.

An Unorthodox Orthodox Iconographer

If such positive, joyful images of Jesus provide psychological and emotional support for so many different people, why are they so hard to find and why are there so few of them? I believe they may be as inspiring and healing as traditional icons. Both kinds of images should have a place in the life of the Church.

I was delighted to receive support for my view from one of America's foremost iconographers, Robert Lentz, of San Francisco, staff artist for the *New Oxford Review* and a member of the Byzantine Rite Roman Catholic Church. Lentz says he grew up with icons and a Russian grandmother. When he had finished college, he returned to those haunting images of his youth. Encouraged by an Orthodox pastor, and later studying at a Greek monastery, he learned the ministry and craft of iconography.

"Icons," he said, "are part of the Catholic tradition. Like the Church, they are timeless, and yet reflect historic settings. Icons are windows into eternity, images of the Kingdom. They belong to the prophetic dimension of the Church. It is, therefore, with great reverence that the iconographer takes brush in hand."

For many years Lentz painted only icons of Orthodox saints of the East, but, he said, "Holiness seems to crop up in many places as well. I am now committed to depicting both Eastern and Western saints for the ever-emerging Church. The resulting icons bridge ethnic and sectarian frontiers and speak of unity lost long ago.''

Lentz's style is Russian Byzantine, but, he says, "my subject matter is as vast as the Church herself. In the Byzantine East, icons have always been painted of holy women and men before formal canonization procedures have been held. The icons are one way the people of God have expressed their belief in the holiness of these individuals' lives. As a Byzantine Rite iconographer, I continue this ancient practice of my tradition.''

Lentz says he is "especially committed to the depiction of our new martyrs—be they from the camps of Siberia, the gas chambers of Europe, or the jungles of Latin America—who have struggled heroically for the Kingdom of God.''

Lentz has done pioneering work in iconography. He paints modern icons of persons he considers to be saints, including an icon of Dorothy Day of New York, holding a copy of *The Catholic Worker*, the martyred Oscar Romero of the Americas, and Martin Luther King, Jr., of Georgia, holding a declaration: "How long will justice be crucified and truth buried?''

Recently, at the request of the monks of the New Skete Orthodox Monastery in Cambridge, New York, Lentz completed a beautiful icon of St. Francis and St. Clare together in a quite unusual way—unusual because Francis' left hand is reaching out and touching Clare's right hand, and the figures in traditional icons rarely show affection. Interestingly, the monks of New Skete are former Byzantine Rite Franciscans who joined the Orthodox Church in America a few years ago but never lost their affection and reverence for SS. Francis and Clare.

In June 1984, the *New Oxford Review* printed an icon

done by Lentz in the traditional Byzantine style. The icon depicts Christ as a black man, bearing in his left hand this passage from Scripture: "Whatsoever you did to the least of my sisters and brothers you did to me." The icon is titled "Jesus Christ, Liberator."

In an accompanying article, Lentz observed that Byzantine iconography "is strictly governed by theological considerations. Everything in an icon must conform to the Bible, the historical events in a saint's life, and the other elements of tradition (tradition meaning the way things have been done for a long time). Since icons have never been painted of Jesus Christ as a black man, this definition would prevent such an icon from ever being painted. In a theological sense, however, 'tradition' means the life of the Holy Spirit in the Church, something that is ongoing. The life of the Holy Spirit within the Church has not ceased in our day. An iconographer must look forward as well as backward, respecting the canons of iconography, but also attending to the signs of his own time. To live in the past and refuse to look for God's continuing revelation is to serve an idol rather than the living God."

Lentz observed that people are often surprised to discover some Russian and Greek icons of Christ that do not look at all like the familiar Pantocrator or Holy Face. In medieval Russia, Lentz said, icons were painted of Christ as Holy Wisdom, with bright red skin, a beardless face, royal Byzantine robes, and wings. He said he found a Greek icon of Christ with a long white beard and wrinkled face, as the Ancient of Days from the Old Testament. He also found an icon of Christ as a beardless, winged angel with the three Hebrew youths in the fiery furnace.

"None of these icons bears any resemblance to a Semitic man of the first century," Lentz said. "Each has a scriptural or theological justification, however. And each has been accepted as a legitimate expression of the faith of the Church."

Lentz observed that "no human being has ever had wings or bright red skin, but a very large portion of our race has black skin. A black Christ should, therefore, be less startling than one that is fire-engine red."

Lentz gave the twenty-fifth chapter of Matthew, containing Christ's description of the Last Judgment, as theological justification for a black Christ. "Those persons condemned on Christ's left hand asked him when they have ever seen him in the many strange and un-Godlike manifestations he has just described: naked, starving, homeless, in prison. They are amazed when he tells them they have ignored *him* whenever they have ignored the least of his sisters and brothers."

Lentz noted that in the lives of the saints, Christ sometimes has appeared as a beggar or sick person in need, and that "the Russian Orthodox people have always understood Christ's presence among the poor and oppressed."

Lentz concluded the article: "Times have changed. New images are needed—as well as some of the old—to express the Gospel in our day."

Blacks have been remarkable not only in their adherence to the Christian faith in the face of poverty and discrimination, but also in their cultivation of a keen sense of humor. So, if I were to visualize a black Christ, I would see him smiling. After reading the *New Oxford Review* article, I wrote to Lentz and suggested he try his hand at painting a smiling black Christ.

Lentz responded,

I try hard to keep all my icons of Christ from looking severe. The abbot of the Orthodox monastery where I studied iconography loved severe icons and wanted us to paint our icons so that they censured their beholders. I am not painting for tenth-century Greece, however.

The greatest temptation for people in twentieth-century America is despair. We are faced with nuclear war, the spread of totalitarian government and official torture, disintegrating family life, a poisoned environment, and many other overwhelming threats to our existence.

Mercy and compassion are in short supply today. Should I paint a Christ who looks like Zeus ready to hurl fire and lightning, or one who said of himself, 'I am meek and humble of heart'? It is the gentle, compassionate Christ who is presented by the prophets and the New Testament. I sometimes wonder if the Christ in the severe icons is not actually related to a pre-Christian god, like Zeus, who slipped in the back door during the Constantinian era.

I have read church fathers who have said we should not laugh, but I have *known* holy monks and lay people who *have* laughed—and have not been less holy for their laughter. Thomas Merton, for one, had a great sense of humor. To depict this, however, is more the task of an illustration than an icon. There is a place for both types of art. But while I cannot imagine an icon with a broad grin or a mouth wide open during a belly laugh, I can envision a quiet smile. Even now, according to an Orthodox friend in Berkeley, most of my icons appear to be about ready to smile.

My own background is the Russian Church, though I worship with Catholics now. I am slowly, step-by-step, venturing out from the strict training I received. There is so much beauty in our [Orthodox] heritage, but so much has been dreadfully deformed by prejudice and cultural politics. Your stance, as a writer, is fresh and amazing. Perhaps it will be us renegades who salvage the precious jewels from the collapsing structure of Constantinian grandeur, and make them available to brothers and sisters from other traditions. In the meantime, we will be called heretics by our own brethren—but, then, Christ was called similar things by his brethren. So, let us be fools for Christ, and proceed with our important work with a joyful smile.

Praying in Positive Images

It is surprising how many Christians, as well as non-Christians, misunderstand icons. Icons are not worshiped in and of themselves by Orthodox and Catholics but are venerated for what they represent. They are more aptly esteemed as "windows into heaven," and inside the church, they play an important visual role in the liturgy. In fact, they are part of the liturgy. They are visual hymns of the most powerful kind.

An increasing number of psychologists currently are experimenting with what they call "positive visualization." Dr. Ken Olson, a Lutheran pastor, clinical psychologist, and hypnotist in Paradise Valley, Arizona, teaches his patients to use positive visualization to improve their mood and mental health.

Dr. Olson relaxes his patients by getting them to actually visualize Jesus appearing before them and touching them and healing them of their ailments and painful memories. In his office hangs a large painting of Jesus, and he often asks his patient to focus his attention on the painting. During psychotherapy, Olson himself frequently focuses his attention on the painting of Jesus.

Psychologists are now discovering what the Church has known for centuries: that imagery—the pictures we hold in our minds—can have a powerful effect on our moods and lives. Negative images can trigger depression and anxiety and aggravate pain and illness.

In a recent issue of *Health* magazine, Dr. Joseph E.

Shorr, a clinical psychologist and director of the Institute of Psycho-Imagination Therapy in Los Angeles, maintained that "imagery is the key to the inner world of the individual" and that mental imagery can be used to help people overcome various mental and emotional conditions.

Author Morton T. Kelsey is an advocate of "praying in images," and he has written a perceptive little booklet by that title for Dove Publications in Pecos, New Mexico. "Praying through images," Kelsey maintains, "can transform the one who prays in this way, and can banish neurosis, depression and anxiety."

Kelsey cites *The Spiritual Exercises* of Ignatius Loyola who, more than four hundred years ago, taught the faithful to hold up an image before their consciousness: the Christ, the Virgin Mary, the cross, the resurrection, the images of saints. "By doing this," Kelsey says, "we open ourselves to the spiritual reality which these things symbolize. At the same time, we find emotion awakened within us. And since emotion is one of the most effective agents of religious transformation, it also works to change us from within."

Through the centuries, many other Christian masters and mystics have advocated praying in images. Kelsey observes that God spoke in images, visions and dreams to the prophets, and the Lord's Prayer, which Jesus taught his disciples, "is nearly entirely in images." Kelsey notes that "among the Greek Orthodox, imaginative prayer is reinforced by the aid of icons, the characteristic images of Greek devotion."

He adds, "How different this is from the idea of many people that God will not understand them unless they address him like a professor of logic, in meticulously worded concepts."

Kelsey believes that "the important thing about dealing

with images and praying in them, however, is that it works. People get results. The use of images not only channels one's energy; it seems to tap resources beyond the individual as well. When destructive and self-annihilating thinking is replaced by creative and hopeful thinking, the structure of the psyche is changed and we become open to a more positive aspect of reality."

He noted that Agnes Sanford combined prayer and imaging effectively in her ministry to the ill, and she described this practice in her book, *The Healing Light*.

According to Jesuit Karel Truhlar, "Christ also addresses himself to the faithful by means of images of him. When seen with the eyes of faith, they can lead the believer to experience the glorified [risen] Christ and his happiness. . ."

Father Lester Bundy of the department of religious studies at Regis College, Denver, is a Western iconographer who does icons in the traditional Eastern way. Writing in *The Living Church*, Bundy said he believes "there is a wealth of spiritual depth to be found in these [Eastern Orthodox] images which could enrich our own Western faith and practice."

He cautions, however, that though "for the iconographer the creation of an icon becomes an act of worship directed to God," icons "are not holy or sacred in and of themselves" and should not be used in an idolatrous way.

"The sad fact is, however," Bundy says, "that much of the art used by the church today is not apt to stimulate or edify the faithful or witness to the Lordship of Jesus Christ. For example, a parish I know of has an image of Christ the King hanging over the altar. The image is made of welded iron painted a dull black, and more nearly represents a cadaver than the risen and triumphant King of Glory. What image of our Risen Lord has been imprinted unconsciously in the minds of several generations of children who have knelt in front of that hollow-eyed refugee from a crematorium, chosen because it was some architect's idea of a nice piece of modern art?"

Father John Buscemi of Janesville, Wisconsin, an authority on liturgical art, observed recently that the Roman Catholic Church has undergone a mild period of iconoclasm in modern times. "There was a period when we thought that we didn't need any visual images or references to identify ourselves, so we stripped our churches, whitewashed the interiors, moved out the statues and removed all decorative things," Buscemi recalled. "Then we replaced them with all sorts of really homely things like felt and burlap banners that had words on them, most times in crooked formation for effect."

Buscemi said that Catholic leaders now are rediscovering the need for "visual images with which to tell our story as a Christian community."

Vladimir Bachinsky, a New York iconographer, observed, "What about the little children? What is there in a bare church to keep their minds on the church? How can you better explain religion and Bible passages to children than by showing them pictures of Biblical events and saints and scenes showing the things they did."

Buscemi looks for a blending of the old and the new and suggests that "we still have to create new images for our period in time, and that is what we have not yet really begun to do."

But, in fact, it is being done primarily by laypeople and amateurs. There is a revival of interest in Orthodox iconography. After the murder of Polish pro-Solidarity priest Father Jerzy Popieluszko by three men in the Communist government, the *National Catholic Register* reported that a picture was painted inside St. Stanislaw's Church, showing the martyred priest dressed as the Orthodox St. George on a horse with a long lance. The lance tip is at the throat of a dragon, which is painted red.

Meanwhile, a lot of laypeople and religious women have been doing paintings and drawings of smiling, laughing, and joyful Christs. And these joyful images have healing influences.

The mind is extremely sensitive to the images and words we feed it on a daily basis. We are familiar with hypochondria, or contracting imaginary diseases.

Sometimes I fear we are in danger of becoming a nation of hypochondriacs. Our news media daily bombard us with images of disease, so many diseases as to boggle the mind. I've had physicians complain to me that every time an actor on a television soap opera contracts or dies of a rare disease, their offices are filled with people worrying about whether they have the same ailment. God knows, there are enough authentic diseases in the world without inventing new ones. A little knowledge is indeed a dangerous thing. If it is possible to communicate mental, emotional, and even physical illness through negative words and images, might it not also be possible to communicate mental health through positive words and images? The early Christians thought so. Perhaps the time has come for artists to try to visualize a happy, joyful, fun-loving Jesus with a keen sense of humor.

If you're an artist, amateur or professional, why not try your hand at painting or drawing a joyful Jesus? Before you start, pray about it and perhaps even fast. The image that grows out of this experience could provide healing and joy to others. Who knows? Maybe some day we will hang icons of a joyful Jesus in our churches, hospitals, and church retreat centers.

Epilogue

I have observed that when an author or a person in the health professions discovers a pearl of truth, there is an altogether human tendency to be blinded by the brilliant light of that pearl, to come to believe that it is the world's best pearl, and to advertise it as having miraculous healing powers. It is promoted as a great new discovery, and there is a reluctance to give credit to anyone in centuries past who saw and expressed the same truth. If one is inclined to egotism, one constructs a new philosophy around the pearl, founds a new school of thought, recruits disciples, and advertises workshops. And very soon, the guru and his disciples become so blinded by the brilliance of their one little pearl that they cannot see, or refuse to see, other pearls.

I do not believe that humor and laughter are cures for everything. A sense of humor is a gift from God, but like any gift, it can be abused. Oscar Wilde had a fantastic sense of humor, but it didn't extricate him from *De Profundis*, and he died a very sick, bitter man. Some of our best comedians, comics, and humorists have suffered from recurrent depressions during their lifetimes, have died from drug overdoses or alcoholism, or like Freddie Prinze, killed themselves. In his last years, Mark Twain was a fretful old grouch.

Humor is indeed a healing tool. But there are many other healing tools. There are healing tools available to everyone, like loving relationships, the support system of an extended family, the knowledge and skill of competent medical doctors, good nutrition, exercise, recreation, moderation in eating, rest.

But what we (including many clergy) all too often fail to recognize is that the Church also has many powerful healing instruments of its own: the many beautiful and mind-calming liturgies of the Christian world, the holy medicine of the Eucharist that lifts the heart and the spirit, the sacrament of reconciliation (confession and absolution), the sacrament of holy unction (anointing both the sick and the well with holy oil), blessings with holy water, healing prayers (especially the prayers of forgiveness), contemplation, songs of praise and thanksgiving, a variety of positive, inspiring, and healing music, clowning, sacred dance, moderate fasting, the laying on of hands, beautiful old icons and joyful contemporary images, fellowship and the collective prayers of godly men and women here and in heaven, the zeal, dedication, and spiritual gifts of lay and clerical charismatics, wise spiritual directors and confessors, monasteries, convents, and retreat centers for the broken and exhausted.

Psychologists keep discovering truths that they are often surprised to find have been built into the traditions of the Church for centuries. Leo Buscaglia, for instance, is a charming psychologist who encourages hugging and the human touch. Buscaglia and other psychologists have discovered the healing power of hugging, touching, the laying on of hands. The ill especially, they say, need touching.

Yet, for almost two thousand years, it has been a tradition among the Greek Orthodox faithful to greet one another—and say farewell to one another—with hugs and kisses on both cheeks. Orthodox Christians always have been very physical and verbal in demonstrating their love for one another. Roman Catholic Italians, Hispanics, and Irish are every bit as physically demonstrative. It is not considered unmanly among them for men to embrace one another and greet one another with a kiss on both cheeks. It is not considered strange for women to act in a similar manner. After all, Paul requested that Christians greet one another with "a holy kiss."

Other psychologists have observed that many of their patients are grudge-bearers and have trouble letting go of their grudges and forgiving people who have hurt them. Christian healing ministers like Francis and Judith Mac-Nutt, Fathers Matthew and Dennis Linn, Barbara Leahy Shlemon, and Father Robert DeGrandis have reported that the health of many patients improves, or their symptoms subside, if they can be persuaded to review their pasts and forgive those who have or are hurting them. They call it "the healing of memories."

They have found that hatred, vengeance, bitterness, grudge-bearing are extremely destructive to a person's mental and physical health.

Jesus, of course, cautioned his disciples to forgive each other seventy times seven and warned us all that, unless we forgive those who trespass against us, the Father will not forgive us our trespasses. Forgiveness is at the heart of the Lord's Prayer.

I know of a very angry and bitter man who recovered from a chronic illness after he determined to light a candle each week and say a prayer for the people who had hurt him. Perhaps the health of all of us would improve if we lit candles in church not only for our loved ones and friends, but also for our enemies, real and imagined.

Confession Is a Powerful Healing Tool

I also believe that confession is a powerful healing tool, and the more regularly confession is made (whether to clergy or to others), the more the soul benefits. Some years ago, the well-known Protestant psychologist O. Hobart Mowrer, who has fought battles with depression, wrote a book called *The Crisis in Psychiatry and Religion*. In it he suggested that the practice of confession in the Catholic and Orthodox tradition is a powerful psychological therapeutic tool, and he questioned whether Protestants were wise in eliminating it.

This sacrament has fallen on hard times in our sophisticated society, but it is good to see Pope John Paul II and Orthodox Church leaders placing a new emphasis on it.

Other recent psychiatric research has indicated that a person's image of God can incline him or her either towards mental health or mental illness. Some religious groups see God mainly as a God of wrath, a harsh, joyless God who strikes fear into the hearts of children and adults alike, a God who is forever punishing people, raining down diseases, afflictions, and accidents on both the good and the bad—on the good to test them and on the bad to pay them back.

Other religious groups have celebrated God as a God of love, a God of joy, a God of mercy, a God of compassion, a God of patience and long-suffering, a God who endlessly forgives our sins, intentional and unintentional, of knowledge and of ignorance.

For far too long, the Church has allowed many of its healing tools to fall into disuse, but now there is a widespread revival of interest in the church's healing ministry, especially to the mentally and emotionally ill. It is my own view that what the mental health professionals have been

calling "mental illness," "emotional illness," and a variety
of other diagnostic names during the twentieth century is in
fact—in a great number of cases—more aptly called "spiritual illness." This spiritual illness often is the consequence
either of the sins of the individual against self and God, or
the sins of a materialistic society that victimizes innocent
individuals.

There are, of course, illnesses with organic causes and
cases that appear to have nothing to do with sin. Paul spoke
of the acceptability of "godly sorrow," for instance, the sufferings of Job. But these cases, too, would benefit from a
spiritual approach. If much mental illness is in fact spiritual
illness, then it is the responsibility of the Church to address
itself to it, and to renew a ministry to all of the tormented
people who are afflicted with it. The medical profession
must recognize the Church as an ally—not as a competi-
tor—in the battle against the epidemic of spiritual illness
that is raging not only across America, but also in other
parts of the world. It is the responsibility of the medical
profession to enlist the cooperation of the Church in such a
way that the ill can benefit not only from the knowledge
and skills of the medical profession but also from the healing tools available within the Church. There is a great need
for more cooperation between the medical profession and
the clergy.

Needed: A National Association for Spiritual Health

Jesus comforted the afflicted and afflicted the comfortable. Some preachers and mental health professionals these
days have been comforting the comfortable and afflicting
the afflicted. What we need is a National Association for
Spiritual Health.

While many mental health professionals overlook the spiritual dimension of mental health, the ill people themselves and their families often search for and welcome a spiritual approach to their problems.

Through the years, I have known many well-intentioned psychiatrists and psychologists, but most of the ones I knew saw religion as a part of the patient's illness, a symptom of the disorder, or as an obstacle to recovery. Few were even willing to consider clergy or churches as allies in the healing process.

A few brave and compassionate psychiatric professionals like Dr. Humphry Osmond and Dr. Abram Hoffer have dared to challenge the claims and pretensions of modern psychology. A few years ago, Drs. Osmond and Hoffer wrote boldly that there is no evidence that the nation's well-endowed, well-staffed, and extremely costly mental health clinics and sanitariums are doing any better in healing and rehabilitating the mentally ill than are the worst and most poorly staffed state mental institutions.

It is not generally known that in the nineteenth century, long before Freud and the parade of secular psychiatric professionals, the Quakers of Pennsylvania operated spiritually-oriented, private asylums for the "mentally ill" that were more compassionate, efficient, well-managed, less costly, and effective in rehabilitating patients than are our modern psychiatric institutions. A few years ago, Dr. Osmond, who was then director of psychiatric research for the State of New Jersey, wrote a brilliant paper for the Huxley Institute, describing how these early Quaker institutions artfully combined a caring spiritual approach with the best medical care of their times. And we have already seen how the monasteries, convents, and retreat centers of the Catholic and Orthodox churches transformed many of the depressed people who came to them into joyful saints who contributed greatly to the societies in which they lived.

In the twentieth century, many clergy have abandoned the church's ancient ministry of healing to secular mental therapists who have happily usurped the role of the clergy. This has resulted in a great decline in church attendance and membership, for if the answers to illnesses of the mind, emotions, heart, and soul are not to be found in the church, why bother to go?

In centuries past, the clergy and medical doctors worked closely together as allies for the benefit of a patient's health—one tending to the needs of the soul, the other to the needs of the body. But in the twentieth century, needless tensions and conflicts between the clergy and the medical profession have developed.

Greater cooperation is needed between the clergy, churches, and the medical profession. It would seem that the time has come for the establishment of a national association for spiritual health that would bring together clergy, doctors, psychologists, nurses, and gifted lay people with healing ministries. Such an association could encourage cooperation between all the helping professions, and the use of the healing tools of both the church and the medical profession.

There are today in America hundreds of thousands of men and women who are seeking spiritual direction and sustained Christian fellowship, but who are having trouble finding it. There are hundreds of thousands of lonely, depressed, and frightened people who have fallen wounded on our secular battlefields. Many are rootless and are searching for meaning and a deeper relationship with God.

A national association for spiritual health could foster the establishment of retreat centers which will take in people for weeks, or even months, if necessary. There is a need for hospitable retreat centers that will welcome hurting and wounded people and make them part of a worshiping, working, loving, playing, rejoicing, healing community over an extended period of time. I suspect that such retreat centers will be welcomed as allies by many medical doctors and health professionals alike.

Viva La Siesta!

There is one other great healing tool that has been largely ignored in the United States, and I am about to propose that it be instituted in North America. I am persuaded that it will greatly improve the health of people, save a lot of marriages in a society where divorce has become epidemic, strengthen family ties, and bring more stability into the lives of our children.

I am proposing that we adopt the siesta—the two-hour midday break from work—in the United States. The siesta has been a tradition for centuries in other countries, especially the Latin, Mediterranean, and Oriental countries, and those societies have derived great health and social benefits from it.

In those countries, people close their shops and businesses at midday and go home to enjoy a leisurely meal with their families and then a nap before returning to work a couple of hours later. Children come home from school, parents come home from their jobs and are reunited. The siesta refreshes and renews the mind and the body and gives a person a second wind so that he or she can confront the problems of the afternoon with greater efficiency. Teachers in Phoenix told me that Mexican schoolchildren who went home for a siesta at noon returned refreshed and were more relaxed and better behaved than were other schoolchildren, who became increasingly tired and irritable as the afternoon wore on.

Many employers are aware that the efficiency of their employees decreases during the afternoon. American businesspeople consume a huge lunch under stress conditions—otherwise known as the business lunch—and then return to work at breakneck speed. By the time the employee gets home, he or she is tired, irritable, inclined to pick quarrels with the spouse, and too exhausted to relate to the children.

Work is indeed love made visible, but you can get too much of a good thing. When carried to extremes, the work ethic can become idolatry. How many workaholics have risen to the top, only to end up disabled, divorced, or dead at middle age? A sane society esteems its business managers and laborers but puts the health of its people before profit making.

I have worked for several newspapers and wire services and have watched, with great sorrow, more than a few of my editors and fellow reporters go to an early grave after suffering painful and chronic illnesses. In fact, six of the seven editors who hired me died between the ages of forty-five and fifty-five. They were all good, honest, dedicated newspaper people who poured themselves into their work, and I admired them all. There are some who will suggest that a reporter like myself would have driven any editor up the wall or into an early grave, and maybe they are right. But I think most of my editors were simply overworked. I suspect that the siesta would have lengthened the lives of my editors, as it would do for many of us.

But, you protest, the siesta was an institution developed in countries with hot climates where the people are lazy or it's too hot to work at midday. Indeed, the word "siesta" has a Latin origin, meaning "the sixth hour," or the hottest part of the day. But the siesta also has been a tradition in some countries with cold climates as well as countries with warm climates, so its origins may be more cultural than climatic.

Perhaps the time has come to introduce the siesta to North America. If it is not practical for everyone to go home at midday, perhaps companies could provide cots for employees who want to take a nap.

Dr. William Dement, a Stanford University professor who is president of the Association of Sleep Disorders Centers, reported recently to a meeting of the association that ninety percent of Americans experience needless drowsiness and fatigue simply because they don't get enough sleep.

"I think Americans are chronically sleep-deprived," Dr. Dement said. "If we were fully rested, we wouldn't get sleepy."

Maybe there are sound health reasons for the siesta.

Cultivate Joy and Humor

A young Christian man came up to me a year ago at a charismatic meeting in Indianapolis and said he was having difficulty finding any joy in his life. He wanted to know how to find joy and how to cultivate a sense of humor.

I told him that it had taken me almost fifty years to find joy and peace in my life, but that I was a slow learner and a stubborn sinner. He had found a great blessing by coming to Jesus Christ at such a young age in life. I told him that I envied his coming to Jesus in his youth, and that he surely would find his joy and peace much sooner than I did.

If you want the gifts of joy and humor in your life, like anything else, you will have to pray for them and work for them every day—day after day. When you encounter an annoying situation, practice laughing it off instead of losing your temper. Train your eye to look for joy and humor in the commonplace.

Margaret West, Benedictine Oblate, writes that laughter "is meant to dispel evil and make fun of the follies of life. We must nourish what humor we have, encourage it, and spread it far and wide. Humor as an emotion is inborn. But a good sense of humor develops in stages and over a life-time. In my own life, I have found that every time I master a fear or anxiety or laugh at it, my sense of humor grows richer and deeper. I once asked a friend of mine when she had learned to laugh. She said, 'I began to laugh when my life was in a state of total disaster.' Humor restores perspective."

Several years ago, Henri Cormier, Congregation of Jesus and Mary, a French priest, wrote a delightful little book called *The Humor of Jesus*. Cormier wrote, "The humor of Jesus is always affectionate, smiling, warm. It comes from a loving heart . . . To have a sense of humor means to be spiritual, to have the spirit. . . True, total humor necessarily implies the presence of the spirit, and the Spirit as well . . . Humor does not condemn; it invites conversion . . . Everyone who draws near to Jesus seems to acquire something of his humor."

Cormier observed that "Jesus never told anyone to lie down on the analyst's couch . . . When Jesus finds a person lying on his bed or stretcher, he usually tells him to get up."

"Seek and you shall find," Cormier reminds us of the words of Jesus. "If we search for God we will find him, if we search for love we will find it, and if we search for a sense of humor we shall find that as well . . . Today, he is knocking at the door of our heart, asking us to love each other as he loved us. Today, it is in us and through us that he wants to exercise his gift of humor.''

The evangelist Father John Bertolucci once reminded a praise gathering in Indianapolis that at the very doorstep of death, shortly before his passion and crucifixion, Jesus spoke to his disciples of joy. Bertolucci observed, ''Jubilation is as old as the church. In the old days, Christians were so joyful that they just went on singing, and Augustine said he had to calm them down in order to give his sermon.''

Bertolucci told this story about one of the most joyful people he knows. When he was a young soldier, this man was in a barracks one day when terrorists broke in, overpowered him, poured gasoline over his entire body, and set him on fire.

The man survived, but he was left blind and his face was horribly disfigured. In time, the man found Jesus and became a counselor and Christian healing minister in a church. People came from all around to see him because he knew what pain is, and could relate to their pain. And yet he was always smiling.

''The man had remembered the voices of the terrorists who had set him on fire,'' Bertolucci said, ''and one day he heard the voice of one of them, and he knew the terrorist lived only three blocks away from him. He prayed constantly that the man would come to Jesus and be saved. That is joy!''

If you want joy, learn and practice the art of forgiving quickly, as Jesus forgave quickly.

The sacking of Orthodox Constantinople by the Roman Catholic Crusaders in 1204 was a great tragedy that deeply wounded and divided the Body of Christ. To this day, some of my Eastern Orthodox brothers and sisters are still bitter over 1204, and refuse to forgive the Catholics for it. But every church has a 1204 in its life, and every individual has a 1204 in his or her life, and the Lord commands churches as well as individuals to forgive the 1204s in their lives if they wish to have healing, wholeness and health. When the Lord commanded us to forgive, he commanded us to forgive instantly, not eight centuries later. And once individuals learn to forgive, perhaps the larger Christian church of all traditions could begin to do the same. If Christians put aside their differences, stood together as one, and recaptured the healing ministry of the early Church, what power on earth could stand against them today?

Our smiling Jesus must weep rivers of tears over the divisions within his Church. Yet he continues to reach out to undeserving people with his healing touch and to free them from their prisons and tombs. He remains the Great Healer. And being a healer, he is also a liberator, the Great Liberator.

Much has been written lately about "liberation theology," but too many see liberation only in terms of economics and political power. The Christian is commanded to feed and care for the poor, the needy, and the sick. But, as Archbishop Oscar Romero of San Salvador declared a few months before his assassination, "The Church does not want the liberation it preaches to be confused with liberations that are only political and temporal." The liberation that Jesus brings is also a spiritual liberation. Christ liberates us from our fears, from despair and sorrow and gloominess, from anger and hatred, from bitterness, grudges, and a vengeful and unforgiving spirit. Christ liberates the poor from envy and hatred of the rich. He liberates the rich from their greed and indifference to the poor. He

Authors and Sources

Adams, Doug. *Humor in the American Pulpit: From George Whitefield through Henry Ward Beecher.* Austin, Texas: The Sharing Co., 1975.

Bainton, Roland H. *Behold the Christ: A Portrayal of Christ in Words and Pictures.* New York: Harper & Row, 1974.

Bombeck, Erma. *At Wit's End.* New York: Doubleday, 1965.

Bundy, Lester. "In the Image and Likeness of God." *The Living Church* (Aug. 5, 1984).

Butler, Alban. *Butler's Lives of the Saints,* ed. Herbert Thurston and Donald Attwater. Westminster, Maryland: Christian Classics, 1956.

Cormier, Henri. *The Humor of Christ,* trans. Society of St. Paul. New York: Alba House, 1977.

de Tourville, Abbé Henri. *Letters of Direction.* New York: Thomas Y. Crowell, 1959.

Duquoc, Christian, ed. *The Gift of Joy.* Concilium Vol. 39. Ramsey, New Jersey: Paulist Press, 1968.

Gibran, Kahlil. *Jesus, The Son of Man.* New York: Alfred A. Knopf, 1928.

Hays, Edward M. *Prayers for the Domestic Church: A Handbook for Worship in the Home.* Easton, Kansas: Forest of Peace Books, Inc., 1979.

Kelsey, Morton T. *Praying in Images.* Pecos, New Mexico: Dove Publications.

Kilpatrick, Dr. William Kirk. *Psychological Seduction: The Failure of Modern Psychology.* Nashville, Tennessee: Thomas Nelson, 1983.

Knowles, Leo. *Saints Who Changed Things*. St. Paul, Minnesota: Carillon Books, 1977.

Larsson, Raymond E.F. *Saints at Prayer*. New York: Coward-McCann, 1942.

Lentz, Robert. "Iconography: The Black Christ." *New Oxford Review* (June 1984), 20–22.

MacNutt, Francis. *Healing*. Notre Dame, Indiana: Ave Maria Press, 1974.

MacNutt, Francis. *The Prayer That Heals*. Notre Dame, Indiana: Ave Maria Press, 1981.

Mandino, Og. *The Greatest Salesman in the World*. New York: Bantam Books, 1968.

Sister Marie-Celeste, OCD. *Clowns and Children of the World*. Reno, Nevada: Carmel of Reno, 1984.

McGinley, Phyllis. "The Wit of Saints." *Vogue* Magazine, April 1, 1962.

Merton, Thomas. *Conjectures of a Guilty Bystander*. New York: Doubleday, 1965.

Moody, Dr. Raymond A., Jr. *Laugh after Laugh: The Healing Power of Humor*. New York: Lippincott, 1978.

Mullen, Tom. *Laughing Out Loud and Other Religious Experiences*. Waco, Texas: Word Books, 1983.

O'Connell, Dr. Walter E. *Essential Readings in Natural High Actualization*. Mount Prospect, Illinois: North American Graphics, 1981.

Olson, Dr. Ken. *The Art of Hanging Loose in an Uptight World*. Phoenix, Arizona: O'Sullivan Woodside, 1974.

Ouspensky, Leonid. *Theology of the Icon*. Crestwood, New York: St. Vladimir's Seminary Press, 1978.

Peale, Dr. Norman Vincent. *Treasury of Joy and Enthusiasm*. New York: Ballantine Books, 1981.

Pope John XXIII. *Journal of a Soul*. New York: McGraw-Hill, 1966.

Redding, Rev. David A. *Jesus Makes Me Laugh*. Starborne House, Box 767, Delaware, Ohio. 1977.

Samra, Cal. "Jesus Put on a Happy Face." *St. Anthony Messenger* Magazine (September 1983), pp. 24–27.

Samra, Cal. "Clowns for Christ." *Liguorian* Magazine (January 1985), pp. 22–25.

Severy, Merle. "The World of Luther." *National Geographic* Magazine (October 1983), pp. 418–462.

Temple, Richard. *Icons: A Search for Inner Meaning.* London: The Temple Gallery, 1982.

Talbot, John Michael. *Changes: A Spiritual Journal.* New York: Crossroad, 1984.

Trueblood, Elton. *The Humor of Christ.* New York: Harper & Row, 1964.

Vanier, Jean. *Community and Growth.* New York: Paulist Press, 1966.

Vitz, Dr. Paul C. *Psychology as Religion: The Cult of Self-Worship.* Grand Rapids, Michigan: William B. Eerdmans Publishing Co., 1977.

Ware, Timothy. "The Fool in Christ as Prophet and Apostle." *Sobornost* 6:2 (1984), pp 6–28.

Weitzmann, Kurt. *The Icon: Holy Images—Sixth to 14th Century.* New York: George Braziller, 1978.

Recommended Reading

There are other books and publications on Christian healing, the monastic life, holy images, and related matters that deserve the reader's attention. Here are some of them:

Benz, Ernst. *The Eastern Orthodox Church.* New York: Anchor Books, Doubleday, 1963.

Bourdeaux, Michael. *Risen Indeed: Lessons in Faith from the USSR.* St. Vladimir's Seminary Press. New York: Crestwood, 1983.

De Grandis, Rev. Robert. *Introduction to the Healing Ministry.* Lowell, Massachusetts, 1974. Can be obtained by writing to the author at 108 Aberdeen St., Lowell, Massachusetts, 01850.

de Paola, Tomie. *The Clown of God.* New York: Harcourt Brace Jovanovich, 1978.

Jones, E. Stanley. *Christ and Human Suffering.* Nashville, Tennessee: Abingdon Press, 1933.

Journal of Christian Healing. Founded by the Association of Christian Therapists (ACT). Dr. Douglas Schoeninger, executive editor. 103 Dudley Ave., Narberth, Pennsylvania, 19072.

Linn, Dennis and Matthew. *Healing Life's Hurts.* New York: Paulist Press, 1978.

Martin, Ralph A. *A Crisis of Truth.* Ann Arbor, Michigan: Servant Books, 1982.

Mowrer, Dr. O. Hobart. *The Crisis in Psychiatry and Religion*. New York: Van Nostrand, 1961.

Nouwen, Henri J. M. *The Wounded Healer*. Garden City, New York: Image Books—Doubleday, 1979.

O'Neill, Dan. *Troubadour for the Lord: The Story of John Michael Talbot*. New York: Crossroad, 1983.

Pennington, M. Basil, ed. *One Yet Two: Monastic Tradition, East and West*. Kalamazoo, Michigan: Cistercian Publications, 1976.

Sanford, Agnes. *The Healing Light*. St. Paul, Minnesota: Macalester Park Publishing Co., 1947.

Schweitzer, Albert. *The Quest of the Historical Jesus*. New York: Macmillan, 1964.

Sharing: A Journal of Christian Healing. Order of St. Luke. 8312 Thoreau Drive. Bethesda, Maryland 20807.

Shlemon, Barbara Leahy with Dennis Linn and Matthew Linn. *To Heal as Jesus Healed*. Notre Dame, Indiana: Ave Maria Press, 1978.

Timmermans, Felix. *The Perfect Joy of St. Francis*. New York: Image Books, Doubleday, 1955.

Tonne, Msgr. Arthur. *Jokes Priests Can Tell*. Vol. 1 and Vol. 2. St. John Church—Pilsen, Rt. 3, Marion, Kansas 66861. 1983, 1984.

Ware, Timothy. *The Orthodox Church*. New York: Penguin Books, 1963.

Ware, Kallistos. *The Orthodox Way*. Crestwood, New York: St. Vladimir's Seminary Press, 1979.

Womble, Rev. Rufus J. *Wilt Thou Be Made Whole?* Little Rock, Arkansas: Christ Episcopal Church, 1974.

APPENDIX: PURCHASING INFORMATION FOR SMILING CHRIST ILLUSTRATIONS

The following illustrations mentioned in this book may be obtained—most of them in color—at various prices from the following sources:

"The Christ Clown," a lithograph by Carmelite Sister Marie-Celeste, O.C.D. Prints, and her book *Clowns and Children of the World*, are available from Carmel of Reno, 1950 La Fond Drive, Reno, Nevada 89502.

"Christ: the Essence of Life, Light, Love and Laughter" by Joyce Martin. Prints available from Mrs. Martin at the Franciscan Family Retreat at 21661 Highway 550, Montrose, Colorado 81401.

Smiling Christ by Lawrence Zink, art director, *St. Anthony Messenger* Magazine. Available from Praise and Joy Annex, 4014 Schuster Drive, West Bend, Wisconsin 53095.

"Smiling Christ" by the late Ivan Pusecker. Inquiries about prints may be addressed to Ivan E. Pusecker, Jr., 13626 Stonehenge Circle, Pickerington, Ohio 43147.

"Jesus Laughing," a color screen-print adaptation by Ralph Kozak of an original drawing by Willis Wheatley. Color screen prints are available in various sizes from Praise and Joy Annex, 4014 Schuster Drive, West Bend, Wisconsin 53095; or from Praise Screen Prints, 11325 Blue Water Drive, Traverse City, Michigan 49684.

"The Smiling Christ" by John Steel. Copyrighted by Providence Lithograph Co., 353 Prairie Ave., Providence, Rhode Island 02901. Available through Christian bookstores.

Smiling Christ by Frances Hook. Copyrighted and distributed by John Brandi Co., Inc., Yonkers, New York. Available through Christian bookstores throughout U.S.

Smiling Jesus with two children, by Spanish artist Jorge Nuñez Segura. Copyrighted and distributed by John Brandi Co., Inc., Yonkers, New York. Available through Christian bookstores.

"My Friend," smiling Christ with young girl, by Frances Hook. Available in plaques and cards from Apostleship of Prayer, 661 Greenwood Ave., Toronto, Ontario M4J 4B3.

"The Listener," smiling Christ with a young boy, by Frances Hook. Available from Apostleship of Prayer, Toronto.

"Our Brother," smiling Christ with four children by Frances Hook. Available from Apostleship of Prayer, Toronto.

Prints of the icons by Robert Lentz, as well as prints and notecards by Lentz, are available from Bridge Building, 739 Clement St., Suite 38, San Francisco, California 94118. His hand-painted icons vary in price. A catalog will be sent to those requesting it.

INDEX